Not **YOUR** Parents'
MONEY
BOOK

Not **YOUR** Parents'
MONEY
BOOK

MAKING, SAVING, AND SPENDING YOUR OWN MONEY

JEAN CHATZKY

Illustrated by Erwin Haya

SIMON & SCHUSTER BOOKS FOR YOUNG READERS

NEW YORK • LONDON • TORONTO • SYDNEY

SIMON & SCHUSTER BOOKS FOR YOUNG READERS
An imprint of Simon & Schuster Children's Publishing Division
1230 Avenue of the Americas, New York, New York 10020
Text copyright © 2010 by Jean Chatzky
Illustrations copyright © 2010 by Erwin Haya

SIMON & SCHUSTER BOOKS FOR YOUNG READERS is a trademark of Simon & Schuster, Inc.
For information about special discounts for bulk purchases, please contact
Simon & Schuster Special Sales at 1-866-506-1949 or business@simonandschuster.com.
The Simon & Schuster Speakers Bureau can bring authors to your live event.
For more information or to book an event, contact the Simon & Schuster Speakers Bureau
at 1-866-248-3049 or visit our website at www.simonspeakers.com.
Book design by Alicia Mikles
The text for this book is set in Triplex Light.
The illustrations for this book are rendered digitally.
Manufactured in the United States of America
0710 MTN
2 4 6 8 10 9 7 5 3 1
Library of Congress Cataloging-in-Publication Data
Chatzky, Jean Sherman, 1964–
Not your parents' money book : making, saving, and spending your own money /
Jean Chatzky ; illustrated by Erwin Haya.
p. cm.
Includes bibliographical references and index.
ISBN 978-1-4169-9472-5 (pbk. : alk. paper) — ISBN 978-1-4169-9473-2 (eBook)
1. Finance, Personal—Juvenile literature. 2. Children—Finance, Personal—Juvenile literature.
3. Money—Juvenile literature. I. Haya, Erwin. II. Title.
HG179.C5359 2010
332.024—dc22
2010008840

For Julia and Jake
—J. C.

For Gunther
—E. H.

ACKNOWLEDGMENTS

This book, like most, wouldn't exist without the work, input, and expertise of a wonderful team of people. My thanks go to:

Sarah Compo, reporter extraordinaire, who contributed great research and also organized and conducted our eye-opening focus groups;

Alexandra Cooper, who edits on paper and from the heart, and who first approached me with the idea of a book for young adults. I am so grateful;

Arielle McGowen, Kelly Eggers, Julia Venditti, Sarah Grant, Burt Laskin, and Steve Feldman for their reporting help;

The rest of the team at Simon & Schuster: Justin Chanda, Dorothy Gribbin, Michelle Kratz, Laurent Linn, Julia Maguire, Alicia Mikles, and Anne Zafian;

Elaine Sherman, my mother as well as a former teacher and school librarian, who offered to write the teachers'/parents' guide and did a wonderful job;

Michael Falcon, Laurie Hosie, Arielle McGowen, Kelly Eggers, David Rollert, Rob Maillie, and the guys at Makibie, my fantastic teammates;

My terrific agents Richard Pine, Richard Leibner, and Adam Leibner; and my wonderful publicist Barb Burg;

Jim Bell, Jackie Levin, Meredith Vieira, Matt Lauer, Al Roker, Ann Curry, Natalie Morales, Hoda Kotb, Kathie Lee Gifford, Marc Victor, Noah Kotch, Dee Dee Thomas, Tammy Fuller, Patricia Luchsinger, Gil Reisfield, Rachel DeLima, Amanda Avery, Lindsay Sobel, and the rest of the *Today* show family;

The principals, teachers, and administrators at all of the schools that hosted us for focus groups and allowed us to pick the brains of their students: Donald Whitney and MaryJo Katon at Case Middle School; Jen Voccola at Central Middle School; Joe Cloherty at Eastview Middle School; Judi Dolan at Mark Twain Middle School; Ron Hochmuth at Alexandria Central School; Diana Knight and Connie Bellantoni at Highlands Middle School; Nancy Taylor Schmitt at Indian River Middle School; Charmaine Tourse and Kathy Bennett at Dolan Middle School; Pat Fontana, Kathleen McGraw, Julie Signor, and Molly Goss at Immaculate Heart Central Middle School; Robert Mercedes and Susan Carr at Bronx Middle School 390; Laureen Mody at Cloonan Middle School; Robert Riccuiti at Emerson Middle School; Yvonne Wood and Jill Groce at Guild School;

And my friends and family, who tolerate my bouncing of ideas, and are always there when I need them: Eliot Kaplan, Elaine Sherman, Robert M. Cohan, Sam Kaplan, Emily Kaplan, Diane Adler, Jan Fisher, Debi Epstein, Larry and Jodie Smoler, Roberta Socolof, Laura Mogil, Ilene and Steve Miller, and Lisa Greene.

Finally, as I said in the dedication, to my children, Jake and Julia: This one is for you.

Contents

WHY YOU SHOULD CARE ENOUGH to READ THIS BOOK

What do you think of when you think of money?

Money is everything because without it you can't do the things you want. Money kind of does buy happiness, because everything depends on it.

—Erin, 12

Whenever I make money from a job, my mom makes me record what the job was, the time, and how much I made in a notebook, but she won't explain to me why. Why do I have to do this?
—Michael, 13

One thing I'd really like to know: How much money does an average American adult really spend in a year?
—Tamika, 14

THOSE ARE JUST SOME OF the things kids around the country think about—or wonder—when they think of money. How do I know? I asked.

I'm an expert on personal finances—which is a term for how real people (your parents, your teachers, and yes, you) handle their own money. You may have seen me on television talking about money (I'm on the *Today* show a lot, but I've also been on everything from *Larry King Live* to *Sesame Street* to *Oprah*!), and I've written six very popular books for adult audiences on topics from saving more money and making more money to getting out of **debt**.* But this is my first book for kids.

So I figured that before I sat down at my computer, it might be helpful to understand a few things. Such as, what do you already know about money? What don't you already know about money? And maybe most importantly, what do you actually *want* to know about money? I have two kids of my own—13 and 16—and so I am aware of what happens to books that contain a lot of information they're not at all interested in. They gather dust under the bed.

That's why I decided to do some homework. For about three months last year I met with groups of kids at middle schools across the country. I asked questions about where the money that kids like you have tends to come from (jobs, gifts, **allowance**?), whether or not you have **bank** accounts, what you think of **credit** and **debit cards**, how much you understand about the cost of various things (from groceries to a brand-new car) and the earning power of various professions (actors, doctors, athletes, the president), how much it takes to be rich, and how the economy works. Most importantly, I listened as those kids asked many, many questions of me.

This book is the result. It's written for you, with the help of your peers, and contains both the questions you asked most often (as well as the ones I thought were the most fun) and the answers to those questions. I hope you like it. For that reason,

---

*__Bold__ words are words that appear in the glossary.

I've made sure there are many of the specific things you told me you'd need in order to read a book like this: fun facts, trivia, real information about how you can make money (and "not just babysitting," as Zoe warned me), and how much it costs to raise a kid like you. There are even quizzes and brainteasers. But I have to tell you: Even more than I want you to like this book, I want you to find it helpful. If making money is at the top of your list, then I want you to put this book down knowing how to make more money.

Why? Because Erin had a point when she said, "Money is everything because without it you can't do the things you want. Money kind of does buy happiness, because everything depends on it."

I don't agree with her word for word. I don't believe money is everything (the people in your life matter more). And I know for a fact that more money does not necessarily make you happier. Once you have enough to live *comfortably*, not like a pro athlete or a rap star, more riches do not put a smile on your face. But Erin is correct that money is a very important tool. You need money to get the other things that you need in life—food, a place to live, transportation back and forth to school or work, decent clothes, medical care. You need even more to get the many, many things you want. And if you don't have money, at least enough to buy the things you need, then chances are you will be pretty unhappy, because life will be difficult. You might not be able to see the doctor if you get sick or injured. You might be forced to live somewhere that's not convenient to your work or your school because it's cheaper. And things like nights out, trips to the mall, or vacations will be few and far between.

That's why being smart about money—making it, saving it, investing it, spending it, giving it away, and understanding why it sometimes drives people to be so emotional or do crazy things—is so important. It's also why having a basic understanding of how this country's financial systems work is key.

See, your great-grandparents and some of your grand-parents grew up in a world where other people took care of their basic wants and needs. They worked for the same companies for many years (often many decades), and when they retired, they received a pension—a lifetime income—from that company. They got **Social Security**, another income stream from the government, to supplement that pension. And they got **Medicare**, health insurance paid for by the government, so that if they got sick, they didn't have to worry about who would foot the bill from the doctor or hospital.

Unfortunately, you (and your parents) don't live in the same world. You live in a world where you are responsible for your own financial wants and needs. Chances are, over the course of *your* career, you won't work for one or two companies like your grandparents. You'll work for twelve. You'll have four different careers. You may be able to afford going to the doctor, thanks to the changes in health care that have now been passed by Congress as I write this book, but you won't have a pension. Instead you'll have a retirement account, and in it will be only as much money as you manage to stash away during your working life. Will you have Social Security to tide you over? Maybe. But chances are it won't be enough to provide you with that comfortable life that we talked about before. That's why, if you're smart, you'll learn to **save** and **invest** your own money, so that you can take care of yourself.

I'm not telling you all of this to frighten you. Actually, maybe I am. Just as you may have gone through DARE programs at school that warn you off drugs, and you may go through a driver's ed course that teaches you how insane it is to text behind the wheel, you need to understand the implications of being able—or not being able—to manage your own money.

Besides, what people who are smart about money soon realize is that while having money may not translate into the utmost happiness or bliss, having money means having choices. When you have money of your own, you get to make the decisions. Not only about what sort of sneakers or blue jeans or smartphone you want to buy, but about what car you want to drive and what neighborhood you want to live in. When you have money, you can decide how much time you want to work and how much time you want to take off from work.

Most importantly, having money gives you independence and freedom. When you have money in the bank, you can decide you don't want to live with your parents anymore (no offense, Mom and Dad). When you have money in the bank, you always have an automatic escape out of a bad situation. When my mother was a teenager, her parents made her take "mad money" on dates. In case she got mad, they told her, she could tell that boy she was leaving and call a taxi or hop on the bus. It works similarly today. Your mad money—your personal savings stash—can enable you to quit a truly bad job or get out of a bad relationship. Without it, you may not only feel stuck, you may actually *be* stuck.

And the truth is that no one—not your parents, your future spouse, your employer, or your government—cares as much about your financial well-being as you do. So even though this may not be information that you're learning through school, what you'll get in the next hundred-plus pages is vital for you to have.

As you read this book, please let me know what you think by writing to me at www.jeanchatzky.com. And while you're there, let me know what questions I *didn't* answer. I'll put up a special section on the site and answer as many as I can.

CHAPTER ONE

The ECONOMY and YOU

Lately my parents have been talking a lot about how to save money and how to move their money around to pay the bills that they have because my dad's job is getting cut back a little bit. So money is a little bit of a situation in our house. We have to think about how we can save.

—Max, 12

> My mom is a single parent, so it's just her and me. She and I talk about how sometimes we can't go out and do things like we normally do. We'll talk about how we can't go out to eat right now, we have to eat in today. Or she'll say, "You can't go to the movies now. But maybe later."
>
> —Brittney, 13

It's The ECONOMY, Stupid.

ALMOST TWENTY YEARS AGO, WHEN he was running for president for the first time, Bill Clinton had a campaign strategist from Louisiana named James Carville. Carville, whose nickname was the Ragin' Cajun, gets a lot of credit for Clinton's victory because he focused the campaign on the economy. He even wrote the words "It's the economy, stupid" on a piece of paper and posted it in the campaign's war room, a sort of mission control, so that no one would forget what they should be emphasizing.

What did Carville mean? He understood that the early 1990s, much like the last few years, and of course the Great Depression, were a time of financial worry for many people. When the economy is chugging along nicely, there are plenty of jobs, businesses are growing, and prices on things that you need to buy every day, like gas and milk, aren't out of control, and as a result most people feel safe and secure. When it is not, people want change—and they vote for change. That's what ushered Barack Obama into the White House in 2008. By making sure that the Clinton team remembered, every day, that the economy was issue number one, Carville and company won the White House.

The economy has been issue number one in the last few years as well. Any time you turn on one of the twenty-four-hour news channels, you are likely to hear about it. But what *is* the economy? What is it *really*?

The economy, simply put, is the exchange of goods, services, and natural resources by people and companies. Goods are physical products. Guitar Hero is a product. So are Air-Heads. Services are jobs or functions that people or companies perform for one another. Cooking dinner in a restaurant is a service, so is designing a website or fixing an air conditioner. And natural resources are non-man-made items that can also be exchanged. Coffee, natural gas, and water are all natural resources. When people talk about "the economy" on television, they are usually talking about the national economy of the United States. But your town, city, state, and region have smaller economies of their own. And the global economy includes all of the different goods and services being exchanged around the world.

I Asked: How is the economy doing?
You Answered:

Well, I know that we're in trillions of dollars of financial debt and that in this economy there's no room for spending.

We're in a *recession*. It's not a *depression*. It's a little before that.

You hear all this stuff about how the economy is bad. . . . I don't really get any of that.

From everything my mom tells us and our teachers tell us, they say we're in a bad economy.

As you can see, when I asked the question, the perception was that the economy was struggling. But there is—at any point in time—a real way to tell how the U.S. economy is doing. We have many ways to measure it, but the main measurement tool is called **GDP**, or **gross domestic product**. This is the value of all of the goods and services in the country. Essentially, it's the size of the economy, but you won't usually see GDP expressed as a dollar amount. Instead it's expressed as a **percentage** and used as a comparison from quarter to quarter or from year to year. For example, you might hear a reporter on a financial news station report that the U.S. GDP is up 2 percent year-over-year. That means the economy is 2 percent larger than it was last year. If GDP is up, the economy is growing, and that means good things, like more goods, more services, and more jobs.

GDP tells us what is happening in real time. Then there's the crystal-ball data—signals, or indicators, that tell economists if things are headed up or headed down. Some of these

signals are called **leading indicators**. They move ahead of the economy. If a leading indicator is up, the economy as a whole will likely be growing. The **stock market** is a leading indicator. It goes up before the economy does. Other signals are **lagging indicators**; they move after the economy. Unemployment is a lagging indicator. It improves after the economy is already showing signs of getting better.

And then there is **inflation**. Inflation is a measure of the price increase in goods and services. You may think higher prices are always a bad thing, but they're not. If an economy is going to continue to grow, prices have to go up and wages need to rise. The key is that neither of those things goes up much more quickly than the other. For example, if prices rise too far too fast, but the amount of money you're earning lags behind, you likely won't have enough money to buy the things you need. And if you—and all the consumers like you—aren't spending, the economy will suffer as a result. Back in the 1970s the United States went through a period of double-digit inflation. The economy was struggling, the Vietnam War had just ended and energy prices were soaring (ask your parents to tell you about the lines at the gas pumps when Jimmy Carter was president and they were kids). Since then things have been much better. Recently, inflation has been averaging about 3 percent, which has no one worried.

Look at a Dollar Bill

On the front, in the top left corner, right under "THE UNITED STATES OF AMERICA," it says in smaller type: "This note is legal tender for all debts, public and private." You'll find the same words on every bill, from twenties to hundreds, and they mean that the U.S. government will back up a dollar with a dollar. And because the government always has, everyone therefore believes a dollar is worth a dollar.

The next question, of course, is: What's a dollar worth? Your parents may chuckle and say something like, "Not as much as it used to be." That's because of inflation, which over time has eaten away at the purchasing power of the dollar. When I was your age, for example, I could buy a can of Mountain Dew (my favorite!) for twenty-five cents in the vending machine at my summer camp. Today the same can of Mountain Dew is likely to cost you seventy-five cents or even a dollar. That's inflation at work.

You Wanted to Know:

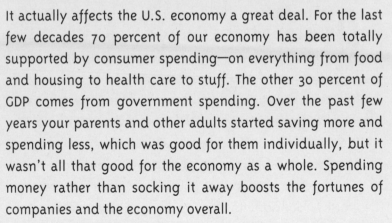

How does the amount
of money people spend
affect the economy?
—Cassie, 13

It actually affects the U.S. economy a great deal. For the last few decades 70 percent of our economy has been totally supported by consumer spending—on everything from food and housing to health care to stuff. The other 30 percent of GDP comes from government spending. Over the past few years your parents and other adults started saving more and spending less, which was good for them individually, but it wasn't all that good for the economy as a whole. Spending money rather than socking it away boosts the fortunes of companies and the economy overall.

We also get a sense of how the economy is doing by looking at these indicators:

CONSUMER CONFIDENCE: This is how positive consumers are feeling about how the economy is doing. It is measured by how much people are saving and spending.

THE DEFICIT: If you spend more money than you have, you have a debt. The amount of that debt is the amount you owe. When the federal government spends more than it takes in—from **taxes** and other sources—each year, that is called a deficit. If the government is able to spend only what it takes in, then its **budget** is balanced. One worry of a big deficit is that it can lead to inflation.

You Wanted to Know:

If the economy is low on money, why can't the government just print more?

—Theresa, 12

I wish it were as easy as that. Unfortunately, though, if you make more money without increasing the value of what's backing up that money, its value will drop.

You're probably wondering, *What backs up our money?* The answer is the strength of our economy and the amount of goods and services that we produce. If our economy gets bigger, our money will get stronger and remain strong. If we just print more money or pump more into the system, its value will drop. Inflation, or an increase in the prices of goods and services, would also occur.

UNEMPLOYMENT AND THE UNEMPLOYMENT RATE: This is another indicator of how the economy is doing. If you're over the age of sixteen and have a job or are actively looking for a job, you are a part of our nation's **labor force**. If you are in the labor force and you don't have a job, you are unemployed. Every month the government conducts a survey to get an idea of how many people are working and how many people are unemployed. In July of 1999, 4.3 percent of the nation's labor force was unemployed. That's about where the unemployment rate should be. At that point few people are worried about it. Ten years later, in early 2010, the unemployment rate soared to 9.7 percent and many people were worried because it was yet another signal that the economy was suffering. When the unemployment rate is high, people have less money, they buy less, and fewer goods are produced.

You Wanted to Know:

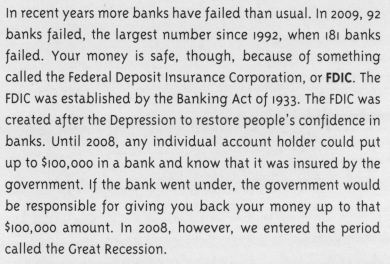

How can you be sure money in the bank is safe today? Don't banks fail all the time?

—Alaina, 13

In recent years more banks have failed than usual. In 2009, 92 banks failed, the largest number since 1992, when 181 banks failed. Your money is safe, though, because of something called the Federal Deposit Insurance Corporation, or **FDIC**. The FDIC was established by the Banking Act of 1933. The FDIC was created after the Depression to restore people's confidence in banks. Until 2008, any individual account holder could put up to $100,000 in a bank and know that it was insured by the government. If the bank went under, the government would be responsible for giving you back your money up to that $100,000 amount. In 2008, however, we entered the period called the Great Recession.

A **recession** is defined as a period of economic decline of usually two quarters or more. Technically, economic growth—as measured by GDP, the value of all reported goods and services produced by the United States—falls over that half year. And during that time, typically, unemployment is rising, personal income is falling, people are buying less stuff, and the stock market is headed down. A **depression** is longer than a recession, and unemployment hits double digits, meaning that 10 percent or more of adults who are looking for work can't find it. Here's a joke from when I was a kid:

Q: What's the difference between a recession and a depression?

A: A recession is when your neighbor loses his or her job. A depression is when you lose yours.

Not so funny, I know. During the Great Recession jobs were being lost. Banks and brokerage houses were going under. And the head of the FDIC, a woman named Sheila Bair, started to fear that we were going to have another period of panic and bank runs, and that that would make an already shaky economy even worse. So she worked to have the limits on FDIC insurance raised. Today, as a result, each individual can put up to $250,000 into any one bank and know that it is insured by the FDIC. What if you have more money than that? Then you need two names on the account—a husband and a wife, or a parent and a child—to double the protection. Or you need to open accounts at two or more different banks.

One more thing: Just because a bank fails does not mean you have to rush to pull your money out. Typically, a bank fails when it can't meet the needs of its depositors. Then the FDIC steps in. It may operate the bank itself as a federally owned bank or very quickly sell the bank to another bank that isn't having financial problems. Unless you read about it in the paper or online, you as a depositor may not even know what's happening. You can still use your debit card or write checks. You can still use your **ATM** card. You just may go to sleep thinking that your money is in the First National Bank and wake up to find that it's in the Second National Bank. Eventually you'll get a new ATM card or debit card or checks, but there's no need to panic, because you're not likely even to feel the change.

INTEREST RATES: And here is another economic indicator. Everything has a price . . . even money. **Interest rates** are the prices that people pay to borrow money, generally from a bank, a company, or another person. They are also the prices you might receive for loaning your money out. If you have a **savings account** at a bank, you are getting paid **interest**. Why? Because when you **deposit** money in the bank, you are allowing the bank to use your money to make **loans**. In return for that, the bank pays you interest. For example, say you put $100 in the bank and your bank pays you 3 percent interest every year. At the end of one year you'd have an extra $3 and change. (The change comes from something called compounding—an incredible way to make whatever money you have today into more money tomorrow. We'll talk more about it later in the book.)

But what determines interest rates? Let's focus on one interest rate in particular. The **fed funds rate** is the interest rate at which the Federal Reserve (the central bank of the U.S. government) lends money to banks. It is controlled by the Federal Reserve itself. Eight times a year the Federal's Open Market Committee meets to decide whether it will raise the federal funds rate, lower it, or leave it unchanged. Many other interest rates—from the prime rate (the interest rate that banks charge their best customers), to the interest rate you earn from your bank on your savings, to the interest rates you pay to buy a house or a car—are affected by changes in

the fed funds rate. But interest rates aren't the only things affected. The stock market tends to rally, or move higher, when interest rates are reduced, because businesses can borrow more money cheaply. When interest rates rise, the stock market generally has the opposite reaction.

The Federal Reserve's Chairman and its Board of Governors understand that if interest rates are high, people are likely to borrow (and spend) less and save more. And if rates are low, people are likely to borrow (and spend) more and save less. They use this knowledge to move the economy to a place where it is growing not too quickly, not too slowly, but just right. (This is called the Goldilocks economy.) Getting the economy to behave like the fairy tale, however, is far from easy. It takes a lot of understanding of how the economy works, and sometimes trial and error. And it's not a perfect science. Think of it this way: The Fed has tools that can help the economy along, but it can't control it completely.

Understanding the Federal Reserve

Managing the nation's money is a big job . . . but it must be done. In the United States that job falls to the Federal Reserve. The Federal Reserve—or the Fed, as it's commonly known—is our nation's central bank.

Created in 1913, the **Federal Reserve System** was designed to keep our country's monetary and financial system safe and stable. The Federal Reserve is made up of twelve banks across the country and a number of branches. These banks and branches are under the careful watch of a group known as the Board of Governors. The board is made up of seven members who are first chosen by the president and then approved by the Senate. The Fed regulates the United States' interest rates and money supplies; distributes money to the country's banks, credit unions, and savings and loans associations; provides financial services to the U.S. government; and educates the public about the economy.

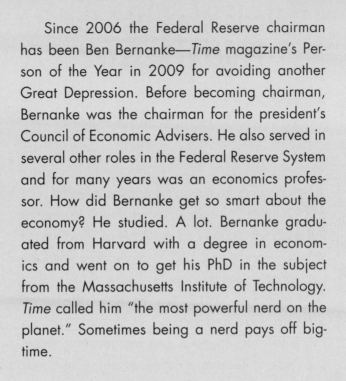

Since 2006 the Federal Reserve chairman has been Ben Bernanke—*Time* magazine's Person of the Year in 2009 for avoiding another Great Depression. Before becoming chairman, Bernanke was the chairman for the president's Council of Economic Advisers. He also served in several other roles in the Federal Reserve System and for many years was an economics professor. How did Bernanke get so smart about the economy? He studied. A lot. Bernanke graduated from Harvard with a degree in economics and went on to get his PhD in the subject from the Massachusetts Institute of Technology. *Time* called him "the most powerful nerd on the planet." Sometimes being a nerd pays off big-time.

CHAPTER TWO

YOU and YOUR MONEY

OKAY, NOW THAT YOU KNOW—MORE or less—how money works in the world, let's focus on how money works in your life. In order to be a financial success—in order to be rich someday, if that's something you desire—you have to do three basic things:

1. You have to earn money.
2. You have to spend less than you earn.
3. You have to save and invest the money that you don't spend so that it can grow into more money.

Think of these like the directions on the bottle of a shampoo: Wash. Rinse. Repeat. Do them over and over, again and again, and that's really all it takes.

I see your eyebrows going up. You don't believe me. *If it is so easy to get rich*, you're thinking, *then why isn't everyone rich? Why are so many people struggling? Why do so many people have financial problems? Or debt? What's the catch?*

The catch is that these steps may sound like easy things to do. But in practice? Doing them over and over, day in and day out, is not such a no-brainer. You need good habits, you need willpower, and you need discipline. Why? Because doing any one of these three things means choosing *not* to do something else that, at the time, you'd prefer to do.

Take the first item on the list—earning money. Earning money generally involves work. (Yes, there are ways to earn money without working, including investing. That's called passive earning. We'll get to that in a bit.) Working means using your time to do something *for pay* rather than hanging with your friends or going on Facebook or doing homework or playing Wii. And whatever you do to earn that paycheck might not be as much fun as those other things. How much of your time you'll devote to work rather than to play is a choice you have to make. But understand: Working is the only way that most people can earn enough money to buy the things they want today and save for the things they want tomorrow.

I Asked: How much do you need to earn to live comfortably as an adult?

You Answered:

$100,000 for bills and food

$1,000

Tons

1 million smackaroonis!

Enough to buy food and clothes
and a house

Actually, it costs about $60,000 a year for a family to live comfortably in America today. But that number varies widely based on where you live. The coasts are generally more expensive than the middle of the country.

The same need to make a choice between something fun and something perhaps not so fun applies to the second item on the list—you need to spend less than you make. Spending money is (for many people, at least) very enjoyable. You may have heard your mother or maybe an older sister use the words "retail therapy" to describe how shopping makes her feel better when she's in a bad mood. For many people that actually works (although it's a short-term fix, not a long-term one). Going out and blowing a few bucks on something you want has been shown to give you the same rush you might get from eating sugar or running a mile. Not spending the money, on the other hand, means you're delaying gratification, putting off the purchase of something you might like to have *right now* in favor of something else later, and that doesn't bring much of a rush at all.

And that third item, saving and investing your money so that it can work as hard as you do, is a difficult habit for most people to adopt. Why? Because again, when you purchase an **investment**, like a **certificate of deposit** (an investment purchased from a bank where you lend the bank your money for a certain amount of time, and in return the bank pays you interest on that money or a stock, which is a **share** in a company), you're not getting something you can hold in your hand or use. It's not like acquiring the new Madden for Xbox, which you can play immediately, or a pair of UGGS you can wear tomorrow. Some investors get satisfaction from watching their money grow, but for others it's like eating your broccoli. You do it because you know it's good for you.

So, we've got:

1. Earn a decent living.
2. Spend less than you make.
3. Save and invest the rest.

The other way to think of these steps is like an equation. If you're going to be financially successful, the number one rule is that money in should equal money out.

If you are bringing in less than you are spending, you are living beyond your means. And that's not sustainable.

I know that sounds pretty basic. You read it and you may think, *Well, yeah.* But I asked hundreds of you what you were learning in school about money and what your parents were teaching you about money, and although some of you mentioned some valuable information, you didn't bring up my three steps or my rule.

I Asked: Did you learn anything in school about money?

You Answered:

If you're leaving a tip, you should double the tax.

Don't spend it on stupid things.

Not much.

I Asked: How about from your parents?

You Answered:

Don't have a lot on you at one time.

Don't make it too important.

You can persuade people with money.

If you have kids, you need a lot more money than if you're single in an apartment.

So here it is in black and white: Whenever you see a person or a family struggling financially, chances are it's because they didn't live by this principle. They spent more than they made—sometimes by choice because they wanted things they couldn't really afford and bought them anyway. Other times they lost a job when the local business shut its doors, and they had to rely on credit cards or stop saving because there was no other way to stay afloat. No matter what the reason, the more you understand about these three steps—and this one equation—the better you will be able to manage them to your advantage and the better your financial life will be.

CHAPTER THREE

EARNING MONEY

I Asked: How do you get money?

You Answered:

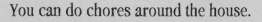

You can get a job.

You can do chores around the house.

You can get an allowance.

You can get gifts for your birthday or the holidays.

You can get a reward, if you find cash or a dog that was lost.

You can sell what you have.

You can *invest*.

YOU'RE RIGHT—ON ALL COUNTS. BUT in this chapter we're going to focus on earning money by working. As you go through school—and you deal with parents nagging you to do your homework so that you can graduate with good grades and get into college and then, perhaps, even go to graduate school to become a doctor or a lawyer or to get your master's in business administration or nursing, understand they have an ulterior motive. Yes, your folks want you to be as smart as you can possibly be. And studying is one way to achieve that. But they also want you to be financially successful. And the more education you have, the more money you are likely to make. Take a look:

Fun Fact

AVERAGE INCOME BY EDUCATION LEVEL COMPLETED

No high school diploma	$25,900
High school diploma	$44,800
Some college	$56,000
College degree	$117,500

Source: Federal Reserve, Survey of Consumer Finances, 2004

Why the difference? The salaries for jobs you can get with a college degree are higher than for those you can typically get without a college degree. In 2007, for example, the average hourly wage for someone working in manufacturing—at a plant that makes medical supplies, for instance—was $17.35. In professional or business services—selling insurance, for instance, or working as a catering manager—wages were more than three dollars higher, $20.59 on average. And working in information technology—such as analyzing information in the computer or financial services field—paid nearly four dollars better still, $24.11. One other big difference between the manufacturing wage (which doesn't require a college degree) and the latter two (which do) is the rate at which they grow. Salaries rise faster in professional and business services and information technology. Unfortunately, salaries in manufacturing don't rise fast enough even to keep up with inflation. Which means that although you may be earning more money at your manufacturing job from year to year, those dollars will buy you less. If your salary isn't going up as quickly, say, as your rent and grocery bill, it's tougher to be sure all the bills will get paid.

Education not only helps you start earning money, it helps you keep earning money. The more school you've finished, the less likely you are to lose your job in a bad economy. In 2009 we saw months in which the unemployment rate for people who had not finished high school was double the rate for people who had graduated high school and at least started college (or gotten an associate's degree from junior college). And the rate for people with some college can be, again, double the rate for those people who have finished college. That means a person who has not finished high school is *four times more likely* to be unemployed than someone who has finished college!

And get this: In the future having that college education will be even more important, because *not* having one will set you apart—and not in a good way. Some 20 percent of baby boomers (people born between 1946 and 1964) received a college education. Nearly 40 percent of their children—Generation Y, which includes people born in the late 1970s up to the early 1990s—have a college education.

And for your generation, the Millennials (born from the late 1990s on), the number will be even higher. Not only will lack of a college degree itself set you behind, but the jobs that are being created in this country demand special, often college-taught skills. For more than forty years we've been losing manufacturing jobs in this country. The auto industry is just one example; plants have been closing every year. Today, still, that trend continues. We are shedding the lower-paying, labor-intensive jobs and adding higher-paying information-intensive ones.

Those extra earnings translate into additional savings and additional wealth. That makes sense; the more money you earn, the more you should be able to sock away for the future. Eventually that will mean a lot not just for you, but for your family. Take a look at the average family wealth by education. You'll see a *huge* difference.

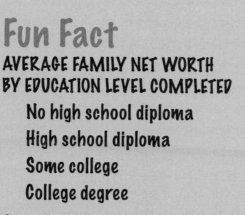

Fun Fact
AVERAGE FAMILY NET WORTH BY EDUCATION LEVEL COMPLETED

No high school diploma	$136,500
High school diploma	$196,800
Some college	$308,600
College degree	$851,300

Source: Federal Reserve, Survey of Consumer Finances, 2004

Interestingly, although you can easily see how getting an education *is* linked to earning money and getting rich, how smart you are doesn't seem to be. Jay Zagorsky, a researcher at Ohio State University, used information from a database of more than 7,400 baby boomers to see how much of a connection there was between intelligence and wealth (the amount of money you *have*) and between intelligence and income (the amount of money you *earn*). He found no link at all between brainpower and wealth, and a very small link between brainpower and earning power. What does that mean? You don't have to be a brainiac or a rocket scientist. You just have to stay in school until you find whatever you're passionate about. Then study that thing until you're at the top of your game. Being a whiz at Sudoku and acing the ACTs is nice, but it isn't everything.

Let's Talk About *Now*

I'm sure that from where you sit, college seems a long way off. What if you want to start earning money *now*? It's possible. Even between the ages of eleven and thirteen there are jobs that you can get or businesses that you can start. Most of this work will take place in other people's homes, where you will be paid by cash or by check. Some of it might be work you can do in your own house. Babysitting is one example, but as Zoe, thirteen, said, "Give us an idea of how to make money—and not just babysitting." Okay, Zoe, here you go:

1. Bike tuner (if you're handy)
2. Birthday party assistant (for little children)
3. Car washer
4. Catering assistant (serving or cleaning up)
5. Computer installer
6. Day camp counselor
7. Dog walker
8. eBay auctioneer (selling other people's old stuff for a commission)
9. Gift wrapper
10. Golf caddy
11. Homework organizer (for younger kids in need of help)

12. iPod installer (loading CD collections)
13. Lawn mower/gardener
14. Leaf raker
15. Math (or other subject) tutor
16. Mother's helper
17. Newspaper carrier
18. Party server
19. Pet sitter
20. Photo organizer (inputting and categorizing photos online)
21. Plant sitter
22. PowerPoint presentation designer
23. Snow shoveler
24. Stationery/holiday card/business card designer
25. Video editor (helping adults post on YouTube, etc.)
26. Website designer

You Wanted to Know:

Why do people have to be a certain age in order to legally work for money? And what is the maximum a child can earn a year in a job?

—Shanthaly, 13

The Fair Labor Standards Act, which limits the age at which you can start working and the number of hours you can put in on the job, wasn't created to prevent you from making the big bucks. It was put in place to protect you. Under this act the government promises to ensure that young people can work, but that the work they do is safe and does not harm their health, well-being, or education. The good news is that according to the Department of Labor, there is no maximum amount that a minor can earn per year.

It's also important to know that for ninety calendar days from your first day of work, your new boss has the right to pay you what's called subminimum wage. Subminimum wage is any amount above $4.25. When the ninety days are up, or when the worker reaches the age of twenty—whichever comes first—you'll be eligible to receive the full federal **minimum wage**, which is currently $7.25. (States have their own minimum wages, but you'll receive whichever is higher.)

Quick Quiz

How much can you earn? The sky's the limit, but let's do a little quick math to see where you should realistically set your sights. Let's take Shanthaly for an example.

At age thirteen she's probably working for friends and neighbors, doing odd jobs here and there. Let's pretend she has a gig walking a neighbor's dog after school each day. She walks five days a week for half an hour, and she earns $10 a day.

QUESTIONS:

1. How much does she earn each week?

2. Assuming she keeps her schedule up throughout the year, how much will she pocket by the end?

3. Let's say she adds another two dogs to her routine for eight weeks over the summer, charging $10 a day for each. How much will she make during those weeks? How does that change her yearly total?

Once you turn fourteen, you can get working papers in
some states, and then you can get a job where you receive an
actual paycheck working in a store, an office, or some other
sort of business. Big **corporations** often won't hire you until
you turn sixteen, so try smaller local businesses. In my town,
for example, I know of teens who found jobs stocking shelves
at the deli and the hardware store, and refolding clothes at the
local boutique, long before they got their driver's licenses.

How do you get working papers? Depending on your
state, they're issued either by your school or through the

Department of Labor. Your best bet is to talk to your guidance counselor, but know that when you go to fill out your papers, you'll need a record of your most recent physical (it will need to have been conducted within the last year) as well as proof of age (your birth certificate and/or school ID), and your parent or guardian will need to sign the papers. If you lose your papers, you can get another copy from the office that issued it.

Finally, depending on your age, there are restrictions on the type of work you can do—though you can always work in businesses your parents own, except if they're in the fields of mining, manufacturing, or anything considered hazardous by the Department of Labor.

> Ages fourteen and fifteen:
> * Three hours a day/eighteen hours a week during the school year. Work must end by 7 p.m.
> * Eight hours a day/forty hours a week during vacation. Work must end by 9 p.m.
> * You can work in restaurants and other quick-service stores.
>
> Ages sixteen and seventeen:
> * There is no limit on work hours.

You can work in any job that hasn't been declared hazardous by the Department of Labor. (Hazardous work includes operating meat slicers, grinders, choppers, and commercial mixers.)

Meet Uncle Sam

When you start your job, your employer will ask you to fill out a W-4 form, probably on your very first day. This is a tax form where you help the government figure out how much to withhold from your paycheck up front in order to cover the taxes you owe, so that you won't have to come up with the money on tax day. You'll probably want to claim zero or one.

If you expect to earn less than $800 for the year—or you had a job previously and owed no federal taxes—write the word "Exempt" on line 7. When you see your paycheck, you may notice that in addition to having taxes subtracted, you've lost money to other deductions, like Social Security and Medicare. That's the price we pay for living in this country.

Once you are officially on someone else's payroll, you will notice a difference in your paycheck. I'm sorry to be the one to have to break this news to you, but it is going to get smaller. And you can thank Uncle Sam—a.k.a. the tax man—for that. You may be used to earning a flat $8 an hour for your work babysitting and pocketing the full $32 for four hours' work. Now say you get a job in a sporting goods store. You are working for the national minimum wage, which is $7.25. If you work fifteen hours a week and receive a paycheck every two weeks, your **gross pay**, which is your income before taxes are taken out, is $217.50. But your net income will be less. Following is an example of an **earnings statement**.

EARNINGS STATEMENT

YOUR COMPANY, INC.
27 MAIN STREET
AVERAGEVILLE, ANYSTATE 10000

Pay Period: 7/15/2009
to 7/28/2009
Pay Date: 7/30/2009

Employee Number: 0002
Department Number: 2
Social Security Number: XXX-XX-8021
Marital Status: Single
Number of Allowances: 00
Rate: 00

Jane Doe
15 Riverwatch Lane
Averageville, Anystate
10000

These are taxes taken out of the paycheck that go to the government.

	HOURS AND EARNINGS		TAXES AND DEDUCTIONS		
Description	Hours This Period	Year-To-Date	Description	This Period	Year-to-Date
SALARY	1153.85	18461.60	FICA	88.27	1412.31
			FED WT	125.46	2111.94
			NY ST	45.39	726.24
			NY DIS	1.20	19.20

Gross Pay Year-to-Date	Gross Pay This Period	Total Deductions This Period	Net Pay This Period
$18,461.60	$1,153.85	$260.32	$893.53

This is the amount Jane has been paid so far this year *before* taxes were taken out.

This is the amount Jane is paid during this pay period before taxes are taken out.

This is the amount being taken out for taxes this pay period.

This is the amount Jane is paid this pay period *after* taxes are taken out.

YOUR COMPANY, INC.   Check Number: XXXXXX
27 MAIN STREET   Check Date: 7/30/2009
AVERAGEVILLE, ANYSTATE 10000

PAY ***Eight hundred ninety-three dollars and fifty-three cents
***$893.53

Pay to the Order of: Jane Doe
                     15 Riverwatch Lane
                     Averageville, Anystate 10000

It hurts, doesn't it? I remember the first time I got a paycheck—I was a salesclerk at Kelly Mike's Sporting Goods in Wheeling, West Virginia, where I grew up. Minimum wage then was $3.10, and still I remember thinking, *WHO TOOK ALL MY MONEY?!?* The good news is that when you file your taxes—and as a working person, you will need to file taxes—you'll probably get some or all of that money back. (We'll talk about what to do with it in a moment.)

Soon after the end of the year your employer will give you a W-2 statement, which will show how much you received in wages and how much you paid out in taxes. If you make more than $9,350 in 2010, you will be *required* to file a federal **income tax** return. If you make less than that, you don't have to file taxes, but you will want to. Why? It's the only way to get a refund of the money you overpaid to the government. Filing will be easier, and free, if you do it electronically using a service called Free File, which you can access through the IRS website at IRS.gov. You'll be able to use a 1040EZ form (the easiest method of filing), and you can tell the government to direct-deposit your refund into your bank account. This way you'll get your money back in less than two weeks. If you have them send you the money through the mail, you'll have to wait nearly two months!

If you have your own business (walking dogs, delivering newspapers, watering plants, even babysitting) and you earn more than $400 a year, you're supposed to pay taxes as well—but nobody is going to hand you a W-2 form. Instead, you should file a Schedule C to report that self-employment income. Now, I know that many teens who babysit or do these other jobs don't report this money, just like many parents don't report it when they pay more than $400 a year to housekeepers or babysitters. But both are required by law.

If you're doing one of the jobs I mentioned, you are self-employed, and it's your responsibility to keep track of how much you earn. You can minimize the taxes you owe by keeping track of how much money you spend to keep your business running. Say you are a dog walker—the money you use to buy your leashes and dog treats, as well as to advertise, etc., are your business expenses. If you earn $700 a year through your business, but you spend $400 to get it up and running, you are making only $300 a year, and so you won't be taxed. But only once you've calculated how much you earned and what your expenses were can you actually determine that. So keeping records is very important.

CHAPTER FOUR

SPENDING MONEY

You Wanted to Know:

How much would a kid need in a year, including going out on weekends, clothes, school supplies, and snacks?
—Tiana, 13

FOOD, CLOTHES, doctor appointments, school supplies . . . let's face it, your parents spend a lot of money on you. How much exactly? For 2008 the U.S. Department of

Agriculture estimated that child care expenses for middle-income two-parent families ranged from $11,610 to $13,480. This amount may go up or down depending on how much money your parents make, whether or not you have siblings, whether you have two parents or one, where you live, and how old you are.

So where exactly is all that money going? About one third of that money is going toward putting a roof over your head. About one sixth goes toward child care and education. This is everything from paying for babysitters to buying your school supplies. Another one sixth pays for food. And the rest goes toward the family car, health care (from physicals to getting your teeth cleaned), clothes, and everything else.

Even though your parents might pay for the things you need, you're probably going to have a lot of wants, too, and I'm sorry to say, they probably won't be paying for all of these. In a recent survey most teens said they have about $30 a week to spend on themselves. That adds up to $1,560 a year. Here's what they spend it on: video games, movie tickets, some clothing items, trips with friends, snacks and candy, music, gifts, electronics, jewelry and accessories, makeup, magazines, comics, and collectible cards.

Eeeew, Gross!
Can Your Money
Make You Sick?

The term "filthy rich" comes from the Bible—it was "filthy lucre" originally, and it was used to describe money earned dishonestly. More recently, however, we've discovered our paper money often is filthy. It carries germs that can actually make you sick.

The guiltiest parties are ones, fives, tens, and twenties. According to reporters at SmartMoney.com, the flu virus by itself can last on paper money for about an hour. But if a little human mucus is in the mix (I told you it was gross, but think about it, you wipe your nose on the back of your hand, then use that same hand to pull out the bill that buys you a Coke), it protects the virus, which can then live for anywhere from ten to seventeen days. That gives it plenty of time to move from the wallet and hands of a sick person into those of a previously healthy one. And if the healthy one just so happens to take the hand that handled the money (now contaminated with germs) and put it in his or her mouth—boom. Transfer complete.

So, what do you do? Coins are an option—the metals in them block viruses—but they're a little inconvenient. New bills are also preferable. The ink contains an antifungal that prevents viruses, but it wears away after time. And credit cards aren't touched by as many people, so they don't get as many germs. But the best solution is to listen to your mother, President Obama, and Elmo, all of whom are saying the same thing: Wash your hands. Use sanitizing gel. And when you sneeze, cover your mouth with your arm rather than your hand. The stranger who handles your money next will thank you.

The Bank of Mom and Dad

My dad, he calls himself an ATM because we always come up to him and ask him for money, and well, it depends if it's a reasonable amount or not. Let's say it's for lunch money. He'll give us $5. But let's say we want to buy a video game. He tells us to use money of our own.

—Sean, 13

For doing the dishes, I will probably get $5. For cleaning my room, I'll get more because my room is very messy. So at the end of the week it will all add up to money in my pocket for the weekend to go out with my friends and stuff.

—Dan, 12

If you're not working for your money—and if it's not your birthday or the holidays—chances are any money you have comes right out of your parents' pockets. Some parents give their kids money when they ask for it—or when they see a need. Others do it on a regular or semiregular schedule in the form of an allowance.

Fun Fact
ALLOWANCES IN THE UNITED STATES

25% of teens receive	**$0**
6% receive	**$1–$19 a month**
24% receive	**$20–$49 a month**
21% receive	**$50–$99 a month**
23% receive	**$100 or more a month**

Source: Charles Schwab, Parents and Money Survey, 2008

Some parents tie allowances to chores (as in, if you empty the dishwasher every night, they'll give you $5 a week). Other parents prefer to use an allowance as a reward for good grades. If I were you, I'd be wondering two things. First, if I don't get an allowance right now, how can I get my parents to start one? And second, if I do get an allowance right now, how can I get my parents to give me a raise?

How to Get a Raise in Your Allowance

Let me explain to you my theory on allowances. (You should feel free to turn down the corner of this page and show this section to your parents to get them on board.) I think that the very best way to teach kids about money is to put some in their hands and force them to use it by making choices about things they actually care about. I'm a parent, so I know I would certainly prefer my kids to work for the money they have. But up until about age eleven, when babysitting and dog-walking work kicks in, that's a tall order. So the best way to make sure your kids have money is to give them some on a regular schedule, like a paycheck.

In order for this to work properly, the money has to come with responsibilities attached—not necessarily chores or grades, but a list of things your parents are no longer willing to buy for you that you are going to buy yourself out of your allowance. Snacks or lunch in the cafeteria, movie tickets, video games, all of these things are fair game. When your parents start an allowance, they need to compile a list of all of the things they used to buy that you are now going to be responsible for paying for yourself. Your allowance should be large enough to cover a reasonable amount of these things—but not so large that you can buy unlimited quantities. Part of what an allowance is supposed to teach you is that money is a limited resource, and that once you blow a week's worth in a day, it's gone until you get paid the next time.

My kids know this. And recently my thirteen-year-old daughter, Julia, used the information to get me to give her a raise. She explained that since she was in middle school this year, she would be going into our little village with her friends once or twice a week to hang out after school. (I knew this was true because her older brother had done the same.) She explained that if she wanted to get a snack in town, it would cost money, and she'd probably have to nag me for a few dollars every time she went into town, unless I gave her a raise. She knows I hate nagging. She got the money.

But not all the money. I explained to her that I was willing to fund one trip into the village a week, but not more. If she wanted more, she was going to have to earn the money. So she spread the word that she was available as a mother's helper and babysitter and now she has a few regular clients.

I'd suggest you do the same thing. Think about all the times you ask Mom or Dad for money. Add up the amount they give you every week. Then suggest to them that they give it to you in a lump sum rather than in little pieces. Having the lump sum will give you more control over the money. You can decide to save it for things that matter to you. You can use it at your discretion. And when you have bigger sums of money to handle, and you will as you get older, you'll be better equipped to manage it.

Needs and Wants Worksheet

Use this space to make a list of the things you think you need or want to spend money on—things like snacks, magazines, and videos. That way, if you decide to approach your parents for a raise, you'll have an organized argument for why you need the extra cash. Remember to be realistic—you need to show your parents that you understand and appreciate the value of the money you're being given.

Expense	Approximate Cost per Week
Total	$

Automatic Payments

Many (if not most) parents—I have been guilty of this myself—promise their kids allowance but sometimes don't pay up. We know it's not right, but sometimes we're too busy to dig out our wallets, sometimes we don't have the right bills, other times we don't have the cash (and may not want to admit it to you), or after a long day we may just be too lazy. What makes us feel worse, though, is when you come up to us and say, "Mom, you owe me five weeks' allowance." We know you have a point, but maybe it's been four weeks (and we come out on the losing end) or six weeks (and you do). Nobody is really sure. We pay up, but we do it crankily.

As I said, I was a parent like this. But I'm not anymore because I give my kids their allowances electronically. If you have delinquent parents, you might want to introduce them to this concept. There are several ways to do this: allowance websites, prepaid credit cards, and debit cards.

- **Allowance websites like ThreeJars (www.threejars.com) or Active Allowance (www.activeallowance.com) charge your folks a subscription fee to participate.** (They can try both sites for free for a couple of weeks to see if they like them.) Once your folks are up and running, they set up parameters. They tell the site how much allowance you get each week, what you have to do in order to earn the money (if there are jobs attached), and how much they want you to spend versus save versus give to charity, and then the computer keeps tabs on how much your parents owe you. Every week you get credited for your full allowance. Then when you want cash, you send your mom or dad an e-mail through the site or print out an allowance check. If your parents approve the transaction, they pay up—in cash—and deduct the amount they handed you from your total. Your parents, in that way, become your own personal ATM. And because you take out cash only when you need it, you save more and avoid the problem of cash getting lost in pockets or around the house.

- **Prepaid credit cards, like Visa Buxx and Allow from MasterCard, are another option.** Your parent applies for a card for you, then loads it with your allowance (probably once a month, since there are small fees for transferring money to the card). When you need to buy something, you use the card. As long as you have enough money, your transaction will be approved—just like with your parents' debit card. And you can also use the card to get cash from an ATM. But you should be aware that there are sometimes fees for making **withdrawals**.

- **If you don't like the fees (and I don't know why you would), the third option is a plain old debit card.** Many banks offer student checking accounts with no minimum **balance** requirements and no monthly fees. They come with debit cards for taking cash out of the bank—but you can also use them to pay for things in just about any store. You (or your parents) need to open your account at the same place where your parents bank, and it should be linked to your parents' account so that they can easily move money back and forth. Then every week they can schedule an automatic transfer from their checking account to yours in the amount of your allowance. If you need cash and you can't get to the ATM, you can ask your parents for cash, and they can—using the bank's online interface—transfer the amount of money they give you back from your account to theirs. There are two fees to watch out for if you go this route: ATM fees for using machines that don't belong to your own bank (about $3), and **overdraft** fees for spending more than you have in your account (about $35!). When you open the account, tell your parents and the bank that you don't want overdraft. That way, if you don't have the money in your account, your purchase will be declined at the cash register—which might be embarrassing, but it's nowhere near as bad as a $35 fee.

Faking Money

You've probably noticed that today's five-dollar bill doesn't look like the one you saw a few years ago, which didn't look like the one you used to see when you were really little. New bills are designed more frequently than new coins. A new series of bills—fives, tens, twenties, and fifties—was introduced from 2004 to 2008. Another set was introduced in the 1990s. Why so often? Counterfeiting!

It may sound like an old-fashioned crime. And it is. During the Civil War about one third of all bills were fake. And in 1865 the U.S. Secret Service (yes, the same Secret Service that protects the president) was started to try to shut counterfeiters down.

But it's also a very high-tech crime. Computers and good, fairly inexpensive home printers mean that counterfeiting has come back—big-time. In fact, estimates from the U.S. Secret Service suggest that about $40 million in counterfeit money is confiscated each and every year in the United States. For example, just recently two men were arrested in New Jersey for using counterfeit one-hundred-dollar bills. What did the police find when they searched the duo's car? Over $5,000 in counterfeit one-hundred-dollar bills. But don't try this at home. Counterfeiters can get up to fifteen years in prison!

Have you ever handed a cashier a twenty and watched him or her hold the bill up to the light? The cashier is looking for an embedded security thread—it's to the left of president Andrew Jackson's big head—and it's just one of the features added to our newest bills that are designed to make life difficult for counterfeiters. These include watermarks (which are also visible when you hold up one of the new bills to the light), the aforementioned security thread (which glows blue if you hold it under ultraviolet light), and new, more complicated (and more colorful) portraits and historic images.

As with coins, making FRNs (which stands for "Federal Reserve notes," the official name for all U.S. bills) is a multistep process. First, new designs have to be approved. Then they're engraved on steel plates made specifically for the press that prints paper money. You can tell from feeling it that the paper that bills are printed on is different from the paper you typically use at home. It doesn't rip as easily, so it's able to handle going through the washing machine. The paper used for money is a combination of cotton and linen, and it is all made by Crane & Co., a Massachusetts company that also makes writing paper and invitations. Thirty-two bills can be printed on a single sheet of this paper, and the ink on the back has to dry before the front can be printed.

I Asked: What kind of jobs do you think earn the most money?

You Answered:

lawyer
doctor
plumber
psychologist
guitar player

You were right and you were wrong. Lawyers, on average, earn more money than most. So do doctors, but they have very high expenses and are constantly fighting to have their bills paid by insurance companies. The only guitar players who make a lot of money are the ones who work with famous singers or who are famous themselves.

I Asked: Who makes more money—Donald Trump or President Obama?

88% of You Answered:
President Obama
12% of You Answered:
Donald Trump

Oops.

In 2009 President Obama earned $5.5 million, according to *Forbes* magazine—$400,000 for running the country and the rest by selling books. Donald Trump earned $50 million by working in real estate, selling products, appearing on television, and giving speeches. Note: Most of our presidents earn a lot more once they get out of office than while they are in office.

You Wanted to Know:

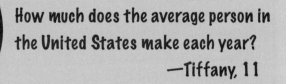

How much does the average person in the United States make each year?
—Tiffany, 11

People who are famous . . . how much money do they make?
—Joseph, 12

The average income in the United States right now is $50,303. Some people make a lot less, others make a lot more.

Here's a list of professions and the amount of money they earn on average.

JOB/PROFESSION	ANNUAL SALARY
Accountant (private)	$65,840
Actor	$60,424*
Airline pilot	$119,750
Architect	$76,750
Artist	$55,140
Athlete	$79,460
Chemist	$71,070
Child care worker	$20,350
Coach	$35,580
Dentist	$154,270
Economist	$90,830
Editor	$57,180
Electrician	$49,890
Engineer	$89,080
Farmer	$49,140
Financial/treasury analyst	$84,780
Firefighter	$45,700
Fitness instructor	$34,310
Industrial engineer	$75,740
Judge	$100,450

*If you can find full-time work.

Lawyer	$124,750
Librarian	$54,700
Model	$30,160
Office clerk	$26,830
Pharmacist	$104,260
Physical therapist	$74,410
Physicist	$106,440
Police officer	$52,810
Postal service mail carrier	$46,970
Psychologist	$90,460
Radio and television announcer	$40,410
Real estate agent	$54,410
Registered nurse	$65,130
Reporter	$44,030
Retail salesperson	$25,050
Secretary (general)	$29,990
Security guard	$25,840
Social worker	$48,180
Surgeon	$206,770
Tax preparer	$35,520
Teacher	$40,770
Tour guide	$25,150
Tractor-trailer truck driver	$38,720
Travel agent	$32,470
Umpire/referee	$28,330
Veterinarian	$89,450
Waiter/waitress	$19,580
Writer	$64,560

CHAPTER FIVE

SPENDING LESS Than You MAKE

Can you suggest some ways—that actually work—to save money?

—Jasmin, 12

You should save your money for college, because if you go to college, you can earn more money and then open your business and be your own boss.

—Grant, 12

I'VE BEEN VERY HONEST with you throughout this book, but I'm going to be brutally honest here. If you want to be rich when you get older, you have to get into the habit of spending less than you make. When you spend less than you make, you automatically save money. And that is a really, really good thing. I recently conducted a survey of five thousand people, and the richest people in my study said that saving more is *why* they are wealthy as adults.

Here's the unfortunate truth about saving money—and if you can understand it now, you'll be so much better able to deal with adult life than many of your parents—saving money is not all that fun. At least, not as much fun as shopping is. This is a scientific *fact*!

Recently scientists called neuroeconomists (neurologists who study, among other things, the way we behave with money) have started using MRIs—brain scans—to actually see the difference. When you are shown an image or picture of something you'd like to buy, the pleasure center in your brain lights up. And when you actually get the item, you get a rush of the feel-good body chemical called dopamine. The problem for savers is that waiting to buy the item, delaying the reward, isn't very pleasurable. It doesn't light up the brain much at all.

Mind over Money

And yet saving money is one of the Big Three. It's one of the things you have to do if you want to have a secure financial life. So what's the solution? Good habits. And mind games. If you think about it, you make choices all the time that are, perhaps, not the choices you'd like to make, but the choices that are good for you. You choose to play a sport after school when you'd rather watch TV. You choose a turkey sandwich from the menu rather than a bacon cheeseburger. In both cases you are rewarded after the fact. When you exercise, you get the benefit of another feel-good body chemical—endorphins (they're responsible for the feeling known as runner's high). When you make good food choices, you typically feel better that day and over the long term as your heart stays healthier, your weight in control.

There are days—I know, I've been there—when you want to be a couch potato, and when you not only want the cheeseburger, you *need* some fries, too. And yet you manage to get yourself to soccer practice or to eat something a little healthier. How? You play mind games with yourself. You make deals. You tell yourself that if you get to practice every day this week, you can blow off the weekend. You promise yourself that if you skip the burger, you can have a Powerade instead of water. Or you trade down to a slightly better choice. You have the turkey sandwich *and* the fries.

Saving money works the same way. You set yourself up to succeed by building good habits, listed below:

- **Save in a different place.** The way adults save most successfully is by automatically transferring a certain amount of their paychecks out of their checking accounts—the accounts tied to debit cards used for most daily spending—into saving accounts. Then they tell themselves those savings accounts are hands-off. You can do the same. If you keep your spending money in your wallet, put your savings in a different wallet, a jar in an out-of-the-way place, or best—the bank, where you can earn interest.

- **Pay yourself first.** Before you spend even a dollar out of your paycheck or your allowance, take the savings chunk and move it out of your spending pile. When you don't see it in your wallet (and can't count it when you're computing how much money you have to go to the mall or for the movies over the weekend), you treat it as if it doesn't exist.

- **Save *for* something.** It's tough to save if you're saving for saving's sake. Your parents know that. They may have had trouble saving for retirement because it's so many decades away that they can't get excited about it, or because they don't know what their retirement is going to look like or where they're going to live. Saving works much better when you are saving *for* something. You won't be able to do it if you're only doing it because your parents (or I) say it's important. That's not very motivating. Instead think about what you're saving for—is it the new version of Rock Band? The new fragrance from Abercrombie & Fitch? If so, cut a picture of what you want out of a magazine, or make it the background on your laptop or phone. You want to be able to see it often. Name your stash: the Rock Band Fund, the Smells-So-Good Fund. And whenever you're tempted to spend some money on impulse, imagine yourself playing the game or splashing on the scent. It'll be easier to walk away from temptation. If what you're saving for is college, you have the same challenges as your parents

have saving for retirement. It seems fuzzy and far away. You can change that by visualizing it. Pick a dream school—you don't actually have to go there, but the place you think you might want to go right now. Get yourself the school's football schedule and put it on your bulletin board, or get a school T-shirt you like and wear it. Stop by and visit if you're nearby, or go online and take a virtual tour. If you can see yourself on campus and that vision makes you happy, it's easier to save the money than if college is just a word for four more years in school.

• **Set the bar where you can clear it.** There was recently a study conducted at Old Dominion University that looked at middle-income people and the reasons they don't save. One big one: Their goals are too high. Many look at the tens of thousands necessary to pay for college and feel as if they won't ever reach that bar, so they stop trying. But interestingly, those people who set the bar lower—aiming to save smaller amounts—not only succeed, they save more in actual dollars over time. The lesson for you is that whatever you're saving for, slower and steadier is the way to go.

Sock It Away

Say you want a new $150 iPod nano. You bring in $30 a week from your allowance and working. If you try to force yourself to save $25 a week (which would get you to your goal in six weeks), you leave yourself only $5 a week for everything else. If that doesn't leave you with enough money to hang out with your friends or do the other things you enjoy on the weekends, you might get annoyed with the challenge and quit. But what if you aim to save $15 a week? You leave yourself with a spending cushion, so you're less likely to fail. And you still get to your goal in ten weeks. Also, if you happen to save more and get there sooner, you get the satisfaction of knowing that you beat the clock.

I Want It! I Need It! I Have to Have It!

Needs are things that you can't live without. Wants are things you'd like to have, but if you don't have them, you'll still survive. Think you know the difference between a need and a want? On the list below check whether each item is a need or a want. Then turn the page to see how you did.

	WANT	NEED
Designer jeans		
Shampoo		
Fruits and vegetables		
Vitamins		
New CD		
Candy bar		
Raincoat		
Video game		
Trampoline		
Eyeglasses		
Graphing calculator		
Toothbrush		

ANSWERS:

	WANT	NEED
Designer jeans	X	
Shampoo		X
Fruits and vegetables		X
Vitamins		X
New CD	X	
Candy bar	X	
Raincoat		X
Video game	X	
Trampoline	X	
Eyeglasses		X
Graphing calculator	X	
Toothbrush		X

Sometimes wants become needs. For example, say you were taking a math class where you needed a graphing calculator to do your homework. That graphing calculator would go from being a want to becoming a need. And you may have to put it higher on your priority list.

Another tricky thing about wants is that there are so many

of them, and some are much more meaningful than others. Your job now, and for the rest of your life, is to learn to prioritize and figure out which of your wants are more important than the others. Why? Because money is a limited resource. You will *never* be able to have everything on your list. (Even really, really rich people tend to want things that are sometimes out of their price range.) The key is to be conscious of what things are most meaningful in your life, so that you can put your limited amount of money to its best use.

I saved up for a skateboard I wanted. I had to save for the whole month because it was, like, $130. I had to do a lot of chores to get to that amount. Once I got it, I felt good because I got what I wanted. And now (a month later) I love riding it 'cause I ride all the time.

—Spencer, 12

> I used some of my babysitting money to buy a pair of expensive jeans that my mom wouldn't pay for. But I didn't end up wearing them after a month or so. I'd take them back if I could.
> —Jenna, 13

What do those two examples show you? Spencer knew himself and his wants better than Jenna knew hers. He understood that because he was an avid rider, he would get a lot of use out of that new skateboard and he would enjoy having it. For him it was an expense worth the money. Not so for Jenna. Maybe she thought she had to have the jeans because everyone else in her group had them. Maybe she saw them in a magazine and thought they'd look good on her—but once she had them, she decided otherwise. The point is that she worked hard for the money too, but she didn't think about the purchase as much as Spencer.

How can you make sure the wants you prioritize are those you'll want long-term? Three rules:

1. **Think about how often you will see it/use it/wear it.** The more often you'll come in contact with the thing you purchase—whatever it is—the more satisfied you'll be with it long-term.

2. **Pause.** We make about two thirds of all of our purchases on impulse. And impulse purchases are often

the ones we regret the most. If you see something you want, don't buy it immediately. Instead put it on hold for twenty-four hours, then come back and see if you still feel as strongly about it a day later.

3. **Experiences trump things.** As time passes, you will tend to lose your excitement over the things that you buy. They break. They don't fit. They are replaced by newer, more exciting items that you want more. That doesn't happen when you spend your money on experiences—trips, concert tickets, etc. Why? Because when you tell the stories of how much fun it was to go on that vacation or see that particular show, you relive the excitement. And when you embellish a little bit (as most people tend to do), you find that your satisfaction with spending money in that way sometimes even grows.

You Wanted to Know:

Why don't we use the barter system today?
—Michael, 12

Actually, we do. In fact, since the economy hit the skids in 2007, bartering has come back big-time. And it can work for you. Say you have the first two Twilight books and you're ready to read the third. Or you have some games for Wii or Xbox that you're a little tired of and you'd like some new ones. You don't have any cash on hand and your parents aren't eager to ante up. You can go to a bartering website. You list the items you have, and the Internet functions as a marketplace that connects you with people who have what you want. (On some sites you don't even have to make a direct match; you get points when someone takes your items, and then you can use those points to buy what someone else has.)

Here are some bartering sites to try:

- www.swaptree.com
- www.titletrader.com
- www.barterthing.com
- www.webswap.com

The 10 Percent Solution

My mom says I can't spend all my money at once. If I get $10, I am not allowed to spend the $10 in one day. How much do I really need to save?
—Sarah, 11

If you can get yourself into the habit of saving 10 percent of all the money you have, over a lifetime you'll do just fine. Now, that 10 percent won't necessarily get you that iPod or that bike or those boots as quickly as you'd like. You may want to save more than 10 percent if you have a particular goal. But when we talk about building a habit of saving, we're really talking about two things—emergencies and the long term. Saving 10 percent of your money over time should satisfy both of those needs.

Let's talk about emergencies first. You need to save for emergencies because in life—in adult life, but also in your own life—stuff happens. You lose your phone and have to replace it. Or worse, you and your friends are playing ball in the basement, the screen on the big TV gets cracked, and your parents say you have to pay for the repair. Or you want to go on a school trip, and that needs to come out of your own pocket. You always want to have a cushion just in case. For self-supporting adults, that cushion needs to be three to six months' worth of living expenses (rent, car payment, grocery money, utilities), which is generally at least a few thousand dollars. For you, because you are not saddled with the same sort of responsibilities, having a couple hundred dollars stashed away would be

great. It would give you a lot of choices and a lot of freedom. And it would give you the peace of mind to know that if the unthinkable were to happen—if you were to lose your phone— you would be able to replace it.

As far as saving for the long term or the future, I often say that you can't count on anyone to pay for your life in the years to come—particularly your life in retirement—but you. That has never been truer than it is today. Back in 1935, when the Social Security Act was passed, Social Security was intended to be a means of making sure that Americans could afford to continue to live comfortably from the time they stopped working, around age sixty-five, until they died. It succeeded in part because people didn't live as long then as they do today. (Men who reached age sixty-five lived, on average, until age seventy-seven, women, until age seventy-nine. Today, men who reach age sixty-five will live, on average, until age eighty-two, women, until age eighty-five.) The days of big pensions (or income for life) that you might earn by working for the same company for decades, as well as the lifelong medical care that came along for the ride, are gone too. So the job of saving for your future, well, it's all yours.

You might read that and think: *Is 10 percent going to be enough?* The answer is yes. You'll be surprised at how fast it can add up if you start early—right after you get out of college—put the money in an account where it can grow tax-free (we'll talk about that in the next chapter), and keep going through age sixty-five.

As you saw in the last chapter, the amount of money you can earn varies widely by the career you pursue, but according to a 2009 survey by the National Association of Colleges and Employers, the average starting-salary offer for new college grads last year was $49,307. So let's start there and watch the money add up.

Fun Fact

THE 10% ROAD TO $1 MILLION (OR MORE!)

- Assume you are making $49,307 a year beginning at age twenty-two.
- You save 10% of that money every year and put it in a retirement account where it can grow tax-free (you may have to pay taxes later).
- You invest that money in a combination of stocks and **bonds** and earn an average **8% return** on your money (meaning that although some years the markets will go up and other years they will go down, over time you'll earn that average 8%).
- When you are **thirty-two**, you will have $76,103.
- When you are **forty-two**, you will have $244,112.
- When you are **fifty-two**, you will have $617,032.
- When you are **sixty-two**, you will have $1,444,780.

How did I figure that out? Not using pencil and paper, that's for sure. I used the Simple Savings Calculator from Bankrate. You can find it at www.bankrate.com/calculators/savings/simple-savings-calculator.aspx. And you can use it to determine how big and how fast any sum of money will grow.

But there are two really important things to notice about that example. First, you in that example *never* get a raise. If you made more money over time, as most people do in the real world, and continued to save 10 percent of your income, you would have much more at the end of the road. And second, there is a big advantage to starting young. If you waited until you were thirty-two to start saving, by the time you were sixty-two and thinking about retirement, you'd have less than half the money you would by starting at twenty-two.

But why should you start saving your 10 percent now? Long before college? Before you have a full-time job? Because right now, when you don't have a lot of financial responsibilities, saving 10 percent will be easy for you. You'll be able to succeed. And you'll be able to see what it feels like to watch your money add up.

Remember how I said that saving money—unlike spending money—isn't fun? Having money saved *is* fun. Watching the numbers in your bank account get larger gives you the sort of satisfaction you might get from acing a particularly challenging test or getting to the next level on BrickBreaker. You've accomplished something. And it will make you feel safer, more secure, more independent, and more free.

CHAPTER SIX

WHERE Should Your MONEY LIVE?

Did you know you can't take money out of your savings account? I asked my mom, "Can I take money out of it?" and she said, "No." I said, "They won't let you?" and she said, "I won't let you because you're going to spend it on candy."

—Jesse, 11

WHEN YOU'RE A BEGINNING SAVER, you generally do store your money at home. That's okay to start, but it's not a long-term solution. Why? Well, it's not safe. If someone steals your cash (I was amazed to hear how many of the kids I interviewed said that their brothers and sisters steal from them), your cash is gone. You may also lose it. Studies have shown that on average families have $90 in spare cash and change in various places around the house. But those aren't the only reasons your money at home isn't secure. One other big one: inflation. Inflation causes the prices of the things you buy to go up around 3 percent a year. If you aren't earning at least that much of a return on your money, then you are actually losing purchasing power—which is the same thing as losing money.

Your first alternative is to put your money somewhere it can earn you interest just for sitting there, while not subjecting you to the **risk** of losing any of it. This is what saving in a bank or credit union is all about. Your second alternative is to put your money to work for you in a place where you could make substantially more money, but you could also lose money. This is called investing. We'll deal with saving in this chapter and investing in the next one.

We save money, as you probably know, in banks and credit unions. Both types of institutions provide insurance on deposits of up to $250,000 per person (banks provide insurance through the FDIC, credit unions through National Credit Union Administration), which means that if the bank or credit union in which you have your money goes out of business, you'll get your money back from the institution that insures it. The difference is that banks are businesses run to make

a **profit** for the **shareholders** that own them, while credit unions are not-for-profit businesses owned by their members. Because credit unions are not for profit, they can give the money they earn back to their customers in the form of higher interest rates on savings, and they can charge them lower interest rates on loans. But they generally don't have the conveniences of big banks, like a lot of branches to visit or as big a network of ATMs where you can withdraw cash. This can be a big (and expensive) deal. If you are going to use the ATM on a regular basis, you need to be sure you're using one in your own bank's or credit union's network. Otherwise you'll be charged around $3 per transaction just for getting your own money out. Use another bank's machine once a week for a year, and you could be looking at $156 in fees! Also, to deposit money in a credit union, you or your parents have to be a member. Ask your parents if they belong to a credit union, or go to the website of the Credit Union National Association—www.cuna.org—to find one they can join.

Quick Quiz

Let's say your mom gets a big chunk of money—maybe she wins the lottery (we can dream, right?) or gets an inheritance from a long-lost relative and receives a check for a million dollars. That's a lot of cash, and there are many ways she could use it: She could pay off a debt that she has, maybe the **mortgage** on the house you live in or the loan on the car she drives; she could save it so that she has money to spend when she retires from her job; she could take your family on a vacation—in truth, she could probably do all three. But she wants to take her time and think about the best use for that money. What should she do with it in the meantime?

A. Put it under her mattress.

B. Put the money in her current savings account.

C. Open a new, separate savings account.

D. Spread the money around among four savings accounts at four different banks, so that there is $250,000 in each one.

ANSWER: D. Because of the FDIC limits we just talked about, your mom wants to spread the money among at least four different savings accounts at four different banks so that she's protected. If she puts it all in one account, she may lose up to $750,000 if the bank fails. And she doesn't just want to hang on to the check—sometimes checks are voided if you don't deposit or cash them within a certain amount of time. Besides, when you deposit money into a savings account, you earn interest on that amount. That means her million dollars will actually grow into more money in the bank, and she doesn't have to do a thing.

Here are your bank and credit union account options:

SAVINGS ACCOUNTS: Savings accounts are basic deposit accounts that you can open, generally, with no minimum balance and no annual or monthly fees, and that will pay you interest. When you put money in a savings account, you allow the bank to lend it to other people, and for that the bank pays you interest, a return that is computed as a percentage of the money you have in the account. There are two different types of interest—simple interest and **compound interest**. Compound interest is better. And the more frequently interest is compounded, the better the scenario works out for you.

- **Simple interest pays you only on the money you deposit— your *principal*.** If you deposit $1,000 and you earn 5 percent simple interest, in one year you'll have $1,050 (because you earn 5 percent on that $1,000). In two years you'll have $1,100.

- **Compound interest pays you on your principal *and* on the interest you've earned previously.** If you deposit $1,000 and you earn 5 percent interest compounded annually, at the end of year one you'll have $1,050. But at the end of two years (because you earn the second 5 percent on $1,050) you'll have $1,102.50.

As I write this, unfortunately, interest rates are pretty low. According to Bankrate (the website you should scan to find the best interest rates when you're ready to open an account), many of the savings accounts at big banks are paying interest of .1 percent (that's not 1 percent, it's one tenth of 1 percent!). As interest rates go up—they have nowhere to go but up—that will change, but you should know that shopping around for savings rates is totally worth your time. As I write this, the best savings accounts are offering interest rates of 1.5 to 2 percent.

Quick Quiz

How much will your money grow? That depends on a few factors. The most important one is the interest rate offered by the bank. Let's go back to the example I used in the last quiz. Only now it's you winning the million-dollar lottery or getting the million-dollar inheritance. You'll divide it among four different savings accounts at four different banks, putting $250,000 in each one (so that you maximize your FDIC protection). You'll likely earn a different interest rate at each bank. For example, let's say the following:

- Bank A is an online bank paying a 1.50 percent interest rate.
- Bank B is another online bank, paying a 1.35 percent interest rate.
- Bank C is a local bank paying a 0.75 percent interest rate.
- Bank D is another local bank, paying a 0.40 percent interest rate.

QUESTIONS:

1. Where will you earn the most money in interest? The least?

2. How much can you expect to earn from Bank B if you leave the $250,000 in the account for a full year?

3. How much will you earn in interest from all four accounts combined after a full year?

ANSWERS:

1. You'll earn the most money from Bank A because the interest rate that bank is paying is the highest. Bank D will net you the least money.

2. You'll earn $3,375.
The Math: You simply take the amount of your deposit and multiply it by the interest rate.
$250,000 x 1.35% = $3,375

3. You'll earn $10,000.
The Math: We already determined that you'll earn $3,375 from Bank B. Now we need to do the same math problem for the other three banks using their interest rates.
Bank A: $250,000 x 1.50% = $3,750
Bank C: $250,000 x 0.75% = $1,875
Bank D: $250,000 x 0.40% = $1,000
Total: $3,375 + $3,750 + $1,875 + $1,000 = $10,000

MONEY MARKET ACCOUNTS: Money market accounts are like savings accounts on steroids. Unlike savings accounts, which often don't have minimum balance requirements, money market accounts typically require you to deposit between $1,000 and $2,500 just to open the account, and maintain that minimum balance to keep it open. Because banks know they'll be able to loan out more of your money, money market accounts generally pay more interest than savings accounts. You may be allowed to write a few checks a month to withdraw money if you like.

CHECKING ACCOUNTS: Checking accounts differ from savings accounts in that they don't *typically* pay interest (more on that in a moment). You deposit money, and because of that you are allowed to write checks to pay your bills. You also get a debit card, which you can use to pay for things at checkout or to pull money out of your bank account at any ATM. This is very convenient. But as I said in the section on using a debit card for allowances, there are two things to watch out for: ATM fees (very expensive if you're not using your own bank's machine) and overdraft fees. When you use a debit card at checkout, if you don't have enough money in your account to cover the purchase, the bank may let it go through anyway, then charge you a hefty fee. You can be charged $35 to buy a $3 magazine or $5 sandwich. The key: When you open your checking account, tell the bank you do not want overdraft protection (you may have to fill out a form to opt out.) What will happen then if you don't have the money? You may get turned down at the checkout counter. But at least you won't get ripped off! There is also a new kind of checking account you'll want to know about as you get a little older. It's called an interest-bearing checking account, and it will pay you (at least, as I write this) 3 to 4 percent in interest for keeping your money in the account, as long as you use your debit card at least ten times a month. The bank makes its money off the fees that stores pay for the privilege of accepting your debit card (generally 1 percent of the amount of your purchase).

You Wanted to Know:

How do you write a check?
—Kim, 12

Checks used to be a much more popular form of payment than they are today. But we still write 70 billion checks each year, and there are times—whether paying for school pictures, the doctor, or the credit card bill—when many people prefer to write a check rather than use a debit or credit card. Here's how you write a check:

JANE DOE
15 Riverwatch Lane
Averageville, Anystate 10000

1570
1-108/210

DATE **January 15, 2012**

PAY TO THE ORDER OF **My Favorite Store** $ **54.95**

Fifty-four 95/100 ——————————— DOLLARS 🔒

YOUR BANK
Averageville, Anystate 10000

FOR **books and magazines**

Jane Doe

⑆123456789⑆123456789⑉ 1570

You Wanted to Know:

How do I balance
a checkbook?
—John, 13

Checkbook balancing is a form of record keeping that makes sure—once a month—that your record of the business you do with your bank (writing checks, depositing money, withdrawing cash, charging debits) matches up with your bank's record. Believe it or not, banks make mistakes too. Sometimes in your favor. But sometimes not. To balance your checkbook, you have to save all your receipts—proof of the business you did with your bank. If you deposited money, save your deposit slip. If you took money out of the ATM or bought something using a debit card, save that receipt. And any checks you write get recorded in the **check register**. Then, when you're ready to balance, follow these steps:

First, make two piles of paper. Your income (deposits) goes in one. Your outflow (debits and withdrawals) goes in another.

Next, take out your bank statement (or print it out if you are receiving statements online—you should get an e-mail telling you it's ready) and a sheet of paper. Number the paper 1 through 8. Then fill in the blanks as follows:

1. Write your bank balance as it appears on your statement.
2. Go through your pile of deposits and compare them to the deposits on your bank statement, checking them off as you go. Add them all up and write the total here.
3. Go through your withdrawals and compare them to the withdrawals on your bank statement, checking them off as you go. If you have written any checks or made any debit or ATM withdrawals that haven't been processed yet, add them up and write the total here.
4. Add lines 1 and 2, then subtract line 3.
5. Enter the total of any fees you were charged by your bank.
6. Subtract line 5 from the total on line 4.
7. Write the total interest you earned.
8. Add lines 6 and 7. This is your balance. It should equal the amount on your account register or checkbook.

I can hear you moaning and groaning already—do you have to balance your checkbook? It's a good idea. I can tell you that people who do balance are happier and have more in savings. And as I said, banks do make mistakes. But many adults (including me) don't do this anymore. They write checks on the Internet using their bank's website and visit the ATM frequently, and as long as the total makes sense, they trust it. The key if you're going to use the nonbalancing system is to visit your bank's website often enough to know if you're missing money.

You Wanted to Know:

Where does money go if nobody uses it?

—Khadijzah, 13

Money that is out of circulation (which means it isn't being used) is stashed in the Federal Reserve banks. Each of the twelve banks has enough money on hand to meet the needs of banks that are in its district. The Bureau of Engraving and Printing, which produces currency, and the U.S. Mint, which makes coins, supply the money to the Fed. When banks need money, they buy it from the Federal Reserve bank.

I know what you're thinking: *Banks have to buy money?!?* Yes. Most medium- to large-size banks have reserve accounts at one of the Federal Reserve banks, and they pay for the money they get from the Fed by having their account debited. When smaller banks need cash, they usually go through larger "correspondent banks," which get it directly from the Fed. The Fed also keeps its money supply intact through deposits from banks in their district. When the banks have more money than they need—for example, after the holiday season—they deposit the cash back at the Fed.

But it's also important to point out that some money is never printed at all. For example, the $700 billion authorized in 2008 to bail out mortgage lenders was not physical money.

After president George W. Bush sat down and signed the Emergency Economic Stabilization Act of 2008, the next step wasn't pulling out the United States' checkbook. To generate money for the bailout, the government sells what are called treasury securities in the open markets. Treasury securities are government bonds. When you buy one, you are essentially loaning the government money, and the government is agreeing to pay you back with interest. They're sold at a **discount** from their face value. You might pay $990 for a treasury bill (a short-term treasury **security**), then when it matures anywhere from a few days to a year later, you would get $1,000 back. The difference between your purchase price ($990) and the face value of the bond ($1,000) is your interest ($10 in this case).

And it's not just bailout money that isn't physical. In fact, a very large portion of the "money" we use every day isn't physical money. Every day consumers use credit cards, debit cards, checks, and online transfers to pay for things. Paying without cash is becoming more and more popular each year. For example, in 2006 noncash payments totaled $76 trillion. And not only are we using paper money less and less, the number of checks (the closest of these alternatives to actual bills) being written each year is dropping too.

Fun Fact

BANK ACCOUNTS IN THE UNITED STATES
   61% of teens have savings accounts
   24% of teens have checking accounts

Source: Charles Schwab, Parents and Money Survey, 2008

CHAPTER SEVEN

SMART SPENDING

DO YOU KNOW HOW MUCH things cost? *Really?* When we went around the country last year interviewing groups of kids your age, we gave them a test. We showed them pictures of things ranging from a new car to a bag of groceries. And we asked, simply, how much? On some items—like the cost of Rock Band 2 and the new Taylor Swift CD—they were remarkably close. In fact, I'd say they were so close that the difference is probably attributable to sales tax. But on other things they were way off. Teens overestimated the price of a minivan by $11,000 and underestimated the cost of a week's worth of groceries by half, and only the kids who bothered to check whether the blue jeans were designer (they were) came close.

WHAT TEENS THOUGHT VS. ACTUAL COST

	What They Thought	Actual Cost
2009 Dodge Grand Caravan	$34,679.99	$23,545.00*
Designer jeans	$70.43	$150.00
Rock Band 2 video game	$52.56	$49.99
A trip to the movies (movie ticket, small popcorn, small soda)	$21.64	$15.68†
A week's worth of groceries	$47.80	$98.36‡
Taylor Swift CD	$17.88	$15.00

*Dodge Grand Caravan base model MSRP starts at $23,545.

†According to the Motion Picture Association of America, the average price for a movie ticket in 2008 was $7.18. According to AMC, the price for a small popcorn is $4.75 and the price for a small soda is $3.75.

‡According to the Bureau of Labor Statistics' Consumer Expenditure Survey for 2007, the average family of four with two children between the ages of six and seventeen spends $98.36 per week on groceries.

The Three Cs of Shopping

Why is this information important? Because no matter how much money you have to spend, now or in the future, you'll want to spend it wisely. For that, you need to know the three Cs of shopping.

COMPARE: Whether you're buying a car, a computer, or a box of Cap'n Crunch, you'll want to understand how much those things should cost. For that, the Internet is the best tool going. Type the make and model of what you're looking for into a price-matching search engine (PriceGrabber.com and Shopping.com are good ones, and I like the ones at Google and Yahoo! as well), and you'll get a range of prices. Make sure to add in shipping and tax so that you get a true total. Now, I know you're not going to head to the Web for every item on your grocery list, but once you start grocery shopping regularly, you'll start to remember that a good price on a box of cereal is around $4. And when you see one for much more than that, you'll know you can do better.

COUPON: You'll also start to learn step two. Coupons—as well as rebates and other discounts—are a great way to save on pretty much anything these days. For store coupons you should hit your Sunday newspaper. That's where 80 percent of them are to be found. But if you're buying a bigger-ticket item, again go back online. First, if you've isolated the store you want to buy from, enter the name of the store and the word "coupon" or "discount" into your search engine. Discount codes for 10 or 15 percent off everything you buy from that site may pop up. It takes seconds and it saves significantly. If you search for the name of the product and the word "coupon," you'll often find an actual coupon that you can print out and take to the store. And what if you're in the store and you forgot your discount code or coupon? If you're carrying a smartphone, search for offers from the store. These days cashiers can just type or scan the coupon code into their registers; you get the discount, and no paper is wasted. In general, looking for and using a coupon will save you an average of 10 percent.

A Penny Saved . . .

When you're searching for coupons, you may think a dollar or even 10 percent off isn't worth your trouble. But if you do it with more than one purchase—like your mom probably does at the grocery store—it adds up really fast, especially over the course of a year or even a month. For example, let's say you find a 10 percent–off coupon for a few of the purchases you make this month:

Four movie tickets at $8.00 each = $32.00/month
> With 10 percent–off coupon = $7.20 each, $28.80/month
> Savings = $3.20

One pair of nondesigner jeans = $40.00
> With 10 percent–off coupon = $36.00
> Savings = $4

One CD = $15.00
> With 10 percent–off coupon = $13.50
> Savings = $1.50

One video game = $60.00
> With 10 percent–off coupon = $54.00
> Savings = $6.00

Total savings: $15.00 in just one month. That's almost two movie tickets!

CALL AHEAD: Lastly, particularly if you are looking for a specialty item, it always pays to pick up the phone and make sure that the store you are dragging yourself to actually has it. This is not as much of a money saver as it is a time saver and a gasoline saver (then again, both of those things have value too). There's nothing worse than wasting a valuable afternoon and not coming home with the merchandise.

My mom yells at my dad because when we grocery shop and there's a sale on mangoes (or something), my dad will say, "But we don't need mangoes." And she will say, "But they're on sale . . . there probably won't be another sale like this." And then they'll fight right there over the mangoes.

—Carmen, 12

The Four-Letter Shopping Word

Betcha didn't know that there was a four-letter word associated with shopping. No, it's not "debt"—we'll get to that in a few pages—it's "sale." There are many people—like Carmen's mom—who have a lot of trouble resisting a sale. Why? In part it goes back to our hunter-gatherer roots. Food was scarce, so only those people who got out early got to eat. Anything that we feel is in limited supply (and we're encouraged to think items on sale are going to move quickly, so they're likely to run out quickly) makes us want it more. Sales also make us feel smart because we are able to get something cheaper than people who bought it before. That's why when you tell people you admire their outfit, it's not unusual for them to tell you what a great bargain they got. But it's important to remember that even when you buy a $100 pair of sneakers for half off, you're still spending $50. If you hadn't bought them at all, you'd have that $50 to spend on something else.

What's the Best Way to Pay?

Tell me the truth about credit and debit cards!
—Kat, 14

Credit. Debit. Cash. When it comes to paying for most things these days, these are the big three in terms of payment. Now, I know that you do not have your own credit cards yet. And most of you don't have debit cards either. Which leaves you with cash as a single alternative. But I also know that when I asked the teens in my focus groups if they had any questions for me, the majority of those questions revolved around credit cards. That's probably because over the last few years this country has had a big problem with credit card debt. Many people spent too much—often tens of thousands too much—then had to struggle to pay it back. I hope you'll understand enough about how credit cards work that you won't land in the same situation as many of your parents.

I Asked: What's a credit card?
You Answered:

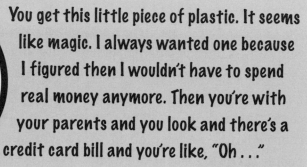

You get this little piece of plastic. It seems like magic. I always wanted one because I figured then I wouldn't have to spend real money anymore. Then you're with your parents and you look and there's a credit card bill and you're like, "Oh ..."

—Meredith, 12

A credit card is something you use so that you don't have to carry as much money around with you. If you want to buy something that is $1,000, you're not going to want to carry $1,000 in cash with you, but you'd use the credit card.

—Lizette, 12

A credit card is a debt card. When you *charge* something on it, you're in debt.

—Evan, 11

> A credit card is a stupid plastic card.
>
> —Devin, 13

> A credit card is something you use to buy things when you don't have money, and you have to pay the money back with interest.
>
> —Maggie, 12

All in all, some pretty good answers. A credit card is, in fact, a plastic card that allows you to pay for things with money that is not your own, but belongs to the bank or credit union that has issued you the card. They're not stupid in and of themselves, but some people use them wisely, and some people use them stupidly. If you pay off your credit card in full each time you receive your bill, you are not charged interest on your purchases. But if you don't—if instead you choose to pay off only part of your bill—you are charged interest on the money you don't pay off. Credit cards allow you to do this. And while it's an okay thing to do from time to time (say you need to buy new tires for your car because yours are shot and it'll take you a few months to pay for them), it can be a dangerous thing to do habitually (say you can't walk past your favorite clothing store without buying yourself a new outfit). This reliance on credit cards is how many people have managed to avoid living by rule number two—spend less than you earn—particularly over the last decade. They spent what they earned, then they spent more on their plastic, figuring they'd pay it back later. But before they knew it, they were hundreds, if not thousands, of dollars in debt.

There are a few things about any credit card that you want to keep in mind. When you're trying to choose a credit card, you can compare cards on these points at websites including CardTrak.com and Bankrate.com.

ANNUAL FEE: Some cards charge a fee each year. It is better to find a card with a low fee or no fee.

INTEREST RATE: Credit card interest rates range from o percent to 30 percent and occasionally higher. The lower your interest rate, the less the card will cost you. Be careful, though, of very low interest rates—they are often just temporary, lasting six months to a year before they jump much higher.

CREDIT LIMIT: This is the amount you are allowed to charge on a card. If you go over your limit, you will be charged an over-limit fee that can be $35 or more. It is best to use only about one quarter of your credit limit at any time. So if you have a credit limit of $1,000, you don't want to have more than $250 in purchases on that card.

The Best Way to Use a Credit Card

The one—and there is only one—very best way to use a credit card is to charge only as much as you can afford to pay off every month. If you charge more than you can pay off, you'll pay interest on the rest. And that interest can add up quickly.

Let's say you accumulate a $500 balance on a credit card with an interest rate of 20 percent. If you can't pay it off in one month, you'll pay $8.33 in interest. If you can't pay it off in one year, you'll pay $100.00 in interest.

That means whatever you spent the $500 on actually cost you almost $100—or 20 percent—more. That's a big deal. You might not have purchased it in the first place if you had thought about the fact that it was going to cost you $600 rather than $500.

Taking the initiative to pay off your whole balance—or as much as you possibly can—every month is something you're going to have to do yourself. Banks and credit card issuers won't force your hand because getting you to pay interest makes them a ton of money. Instead many banks and credit card issuers offer you the opportunity to make a **minimum payment** of only $15 or 2.5 percent of your balance, whichever is more. That means on that $500 balance you could pay as little as $15 per month. Which sounds good, right? You can get the items you want and pay for them over a very long time. The downside is that it will cost you a huge amount in interest. How much?

Pay the $15 minimum on that $500 balance at 20 percent interest, and it will cost you $235.90 in interest and take you fifty months—more than four years—to get out of debt.

If you paid $50 a month instead, you'd be out of debt in twelve months and you'd pay only $51.52 in interest. Big difference, isn't it?

Not-So-Fun Facts

- According to the Federal Reserve, 40% of Americans spend more than they earn.

- Americans currently owe $917 billion on their credit cards.

- Just over half of Americans don't pay their credit card balances off each month.

- Of those households with credit card balances, the average has credit card debt of more than $9,000.

I Asked: What is debt?
You Answered:

Money that someone kind of borrowed and hasn't paid back (you really shouldn't get into debt in the first place!).
—Michael, 11

Money that hasn't been paid and builds up.
—Brian, 12

The amount that you owe someone else.
—Jennifer, 11

Money you pay monthly over time.
—Grace, 11

What my parents argue about.
—Colin, 12

Good Debt and Bad Debt

Debt is, in fact, all of those things. It is borrowed money. It is often paid back over time. And it is often a source of frustration among grown-ups who'd like to be able to pay their bills in full but just don't have the money. But not all debt is bad. Most people couldn't buy houses and cars without borrowing. Many people couldn't go to college without taking out loans. I like to say that good debt is debt that gets you somewhere. It's the house that puts a roof over your head, the car that gets you back and forth to work (not the second or third car that you buy just for fun), the education that lands you the better job. Bad debt is money borrowed to buy things that you want— don't need—right now and truly can't afford to pay for.

Quick Quiz

Let's see if you can tell the difference between good debt and bad debt:

QUESTIONS:

1. Let's say your family's refrigerator breaks and it's not fixable. Your folks don't have enough money to pay for a new one, so they're thinking about putting it on a credit card and paying it off over the next few months. Good debt or bad debt?

2. Let's say your dad lost his job. He was paying for your college tuition each month, but now he can't and says if you want to stay in school, you'll have to take out a student loan. Good debt or bad debt?

3. Let's say your iPod broke. It's something you use every day, but you don't have enough cash to buy another one. You're thinking about buying a new iPod using a credit card. Good debt or bad debt?

ANSWERS: 1. Good debt 2. Good debt 3. Bad debt

You Wanted to Know:

What happens if you don't pay
your bills?

—John, 12

The thing to avoid is taking on more debt, good or bad, than you can comfortably afford to repay. If you don't pay the loans on your house or your car, these items—called your **collateral**—can be taken by the bank that loaned you the money to buy them. If you don't pay your credit card bills, the bank can't physically take anything from you. But it can call you many times and bother you for the money, which is a miserable experience.

Debit Cards: The Newer Solution

Sometimes when you charge too much money on your credit card, you'll have bad credit and you probably won't get approved when you want to buy something. My mom, she had bad credit, so she started paying her debts off. I don't want to have bad credit. I would rather just have a debit card.

—Gia, 12

Many people share Gia's feelings, which is one reason that debit cards are being used more than credit cards in America. A debit card, as I explained earlier, is linked to your checking account. When you pay for something using a debit card, you are using your own money. You won't be charged interest.

Fun Fact

Studies have shown that we spend more when we pay with credit than when we pay with debit, and more when we pay with debit than when we pay with cash. We even spend more when we have small bills in our wallet than when we have bigger bills. Why? Those bigger bills feel more special than the smaller ones. And cash feels more real than debit or credit. So if you want to save money, you should put away the plastic, the fives, and the tens and carry only twenties and fifties.

Let's Talk About Gift Cards

> If you get gift cards, you have to be really careful with them. I got one recently, and sometimes I forget that there's still money on them. If you're not careful, you can throw it away.
>
> —Joey, 11

This happens more than you know. About $5 billion (!) every year is lost in money left on gift cards. Chances are you get your share of these plastic presents. So how do you make sure you get your money's worth?

- **Understand the two types of cards.** There are cards issued by retailers (stores, restaurants, etc.) that can only be used at those retailers. Then there are cards issued by banks that have logos on them from Visa, MasterCard, or American Express. They can be used anywhere that accepts credit or debit cards.
- **Watch expiration dates.** Retail gift cards, in particular, may not be good after a certain date listed on the card.
- **Understand the fees.** On bank gift cards you may face activation fees (often these are paid by the person who

bought the gift for you) or fees for using the card. On retail gift cards there may be fees for not using the card for months at a time. (Your gift card came with some fine print on the wrapper. Read it!)

• **Make sure the merchant is likely to stay in business.** If you get a gift card and then the store goes out of business, it's not worth anything anymore (although sometimes competitors will honor gift cards just to get your business and goodwill). That's one reason gift cards should be used sooner rather than later.

• **Call and complain.** If you have a problem with a gift card, get in touch with the retailer or bank that issued the card (there should be a toll-free number on the back). You should also contact the Federal Trade Commission at 1-877-FTC-HELP. Filing a complaint helps the FTC crack down on merchants that cause frequent problems for consumers.

$10 Starget

$15 Mapple

$25 facey's

CHAPTER EIGHT

MAKING Your MONEY GROW

Our teacher would talk sometimes about the economy. When stocks went up for him, he'd be doing cartwheels in the classroom.

—Blake, 12

I'M SURE IF YOU'VE EVER looked at the interest rates you could earn by putting your money in a savings or money market account, you thought, *Jeez. That's nothing.* You're right. Particularly lately. Over the past couple of years if you put $1.00 into a savings account at the beginning of the year, do you know what you had at the end of the year? About $1.01. It was hardly worth your time.

But it is possible to put your money to work in places other than banks—like stocks and bonds and **mutual funds**—so that you can earn more than you would putting your money in the bank. The hitch is that unlike putting your money in a savings account and knowing you are going to get that 1 percent (or whatever) interest for sure—what investment professionals call a guaranteed return on your money—when you put your money in stocks and bonds and mutual funds, you may not get the return you were expecting. You may even lose money. This is called investing.

I Asked: What does investing mean?
You Answered:

Buying things low and selling them high.

—Henry, 12

Putting your money in good hands.

—Ricky, 13

IDK.
 —Jesse, 11

Putting your money into banks, then adding more money every month to what you have.
 —Jolie, 12

Money that you put away in stocks.
 —Shane, 11

Risk.
 —Carter, 12

Again you are on the right track.

I was particularly impressed by Jolie's comment about investing money every month. Just like saving money habitually—every month—is one way to get rich, investing money every month is another. Many successful investors have money taken out of their paycheck automatically every pay period and then put into stocks or bonds or mutual funds (more on these in a moment), where it can grow until they need it later on.

Let's talk about the most popular types of investments:

STOCKS: Stocks are shares—small pieces—of companies that you buy and sell in marketplaces called exchanges.

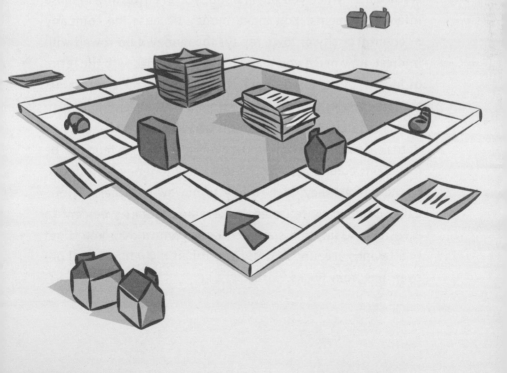

It's possible for you to own pieces of companies you hear about every day (Google, Nike, McDonald's) by purchasing their stock. The value of that stock will then go up or down depending on how well the company is doing and how well people believe it's doing (which are two different things, but which both affect the share price). Historically, stocks have returned, on average, nearly 10 percent every year to investors. Compare that to the 1 to 2 percent you're earning in a savings account these days—big difference!

BONDS: Bonds—let me be blunt—are much more confusing than stocks. There are many adults who don't get how they work. Here's an easy way to think of them: To stay in business, most companies, countries, and even local cities and towns occasionally borrow money. Whenever they borrow money, they pay interest on that debt, just as individuals do on their credit cards. When you buy a bond, you are investing in those interest payments. You make money because the company or country or city or town repays the money it borrowed with interest. How much you make in interest varies with the term, or length, of the loan. Generally, the longer the time frame, the more you'll earn. You also earn more interest for taking on more risk. The U.S. government is very, very likely to repay its debts, so the interest on U.S. government bonds tends to be low. Some companies may be less likely to repay their debts, so the interest they have to pay to borrow is higher. Historically, bonds have returned, on average, about 5 percent to investors. Again, that's a much better return than you'd get in a savings account, but it's about half the return you'll get over time from stocks.

MUTUAL FUNDS: Funds are big pools of stocks or bonds, or both. One of the problems with buying a single stock or a single bond is that if something bad happens with the company you own a stake in, you could lose a significant part of your investment. And the fact that something happens at that company—maybe the beloved CEO leaves to take another job, or maybe you bought stock in a cable company and the government passes a law that all cable companies have to pay higher taxes—is completely out of your control. You can't do one thing about it. You can sell your investment and lose money. Or you can wait and see if the value of your investment comes back (this is called rebounding). Or you can invest in another way. Rather than buying one stock or one bond, you can buy a big pool of stocks or bonds, or both, called a mutual fund, which owns hundreds—if not thousands—of stocks or bonds simultaneously. If one (or even many) of those stocks or bonds has a bad year, you are betting that the others in the pool will do well enough to bail you out. This is called **diversification**.

You Wanted to Know:

My parents are investing in gold. Is that a good idea?
　　　　　—Katie, 13

Your parents aren't the only ones. Lately, every time you turn on the radio, you hear an advertisement for investing in gold. Why, after all these years, does gold seem to be more popular than ever?

Here's why: Gold is typically a good investment when the stock market is doing badly. And from the middle of 2007 until the end of 2008, badly was an understatement. Gold, unlike some other investments, tends to hold its value. That's not to say the price never goes up or down. When the stock market is chugging right along, investors are less interested in gold and the price of gold stocks tends to fall. But unlike stock investments—which can be worth nothing if the company you invested in goes bankrupt—the value of your gold will never go to zero. Gold continued to do well during 2009 for another reason. The U.S. dollar was falling in value compared with other world currencies, like the euro and the yen. Investors bought gold rather than dollars because they believed gold was safer. All of which is not to say that gold is a better investment, over time, than stocks or bonds or some of the other investments. And your primary concern as an investor—rather than a trader, who dives in and out of stocks, bonds, currencies, precious metals, or other markets, trying to make a quick profit—should be making your money grow over years, not over days or weeks. But you may want gold to be one part of your investment mix.

Fun Fact

Stock market investors are often characterized as bulls or bears. Bulls are bold animals who might charge right ahead. A bullish investor believes the market will go up. He or she will charge ahead and put more money into the market. Bears are cautious animals who don't like to move too fast. An investor is said to be bearish if he or she believes the stock market will go down. A bearish investor will buy stock cautiously.

The Difference Between a Gamble and a Risk

I saved up a lot of money and my dad put it in stocks. And it's kind of sad because we already lost it.
—Chris, 12

> If you invest and your stock goes up, you can make money off of your money. If you invest and your stock goes down, you can lose that money. It's a gamble.
>
> —Scott, 14

Actually, if you do it well, it's not a gamble. A gamble—in most cases—is placing a bet where you can do nothing to affect the outcome. What you want to take is a calculated risk. That's where you have done enough homework to believe that the company you're buying will do well in the future. Which, by the way, is not a guarantee that you won't lose money. But you are improving your chances.

Which Money Should Be Invested?

One very important thing to understand about investing is that time matters. Markets tend to move up and down in cycles. So if you have enough time and your stocks do fall in value, you can wait for them to come back before you sell. But if you need to use your money in a shorter period of time, then you don't want to put it in riskier stock or bond markets, where you could lose some and not be able to wait for it to rebound. You want to put your money someplace safer, like a savings or money market account, where perhaps you won't earn as much on your money, but you'll have the comfort of knowing you won't lose it. Here are the general rules:

Short-term money = money you need in the next five years = does not belong in stocks

Long-term money = money you don't need for at least five years = can be in a diversified mix of stocks

CHAPTER NINE

WHY Does Money MAKE PEOPLE So CRAZY?

I Asked: What kind of feelings do you have about money?

You Answered:

Sometimes I feel guilty when I spend it.

—Emily, 12

Sometimes you're happy because when you buy something yourself, you have the individuality where you, yourself, did it. But most of the time you're like "Really, should I have gotten that?"
—Maya, 11

I worry about it. My parents say I don't need to worry about it, but I do. I worry about what's going on in the house budgetwise.
—Michael, 12

You need money mostly to fit in with other kids. You need the right iPod, the right clothes.
—Amanda, 12

IHAVE BEEN REPORTING ABOUT real people and their money for more years than you have been alive, and so I can tell you—both from personal experience and from research—it does make people a little crazy. People fight about money. They get jealous over money. They do things for money—lie, cheat, steal—that they wouldn't do if money weren't part of the equation.

Why? Because money is not just that green stuff you're carrying in your wallet. Money represents power in certain situations—the person with more money is the person with more control. In other cases money represents social status or self-esteem—the person with more money can afford those status symbols that seem to mean so much, especially to teens. Other people equate money with love—the more money someone is willing to give you, the more they must love you. Or so the logic goes.

As many of us get older, we realize (at least in our more rational moments) that money really doesn't have the ability to buy us power or love or friends. But that doesn't mean we don't fall back on this old rationale every so often.

My mom and my stepfather have fights because my stepfather bought a motorcycle and my mom kept telling him not to. She felt like it was a luxury and it wasn't really something they needed. They had three kids already, and my mom felt like it was a waste of money. After two weeks he sold the motorcycle.

—James, 12

But maybe after reading this chapter, you'll also understand that it wasn't really the money James's parents were fighting about. It was about who had the power to set priorities for the family. It sounds like they came to a meeting of the minds in the end.

There's More Emotion When Money Is Scarce

My parents fight about money because sometimes people owe them money . . . or they owe people money and they don't have enough money.

—Dana, 13

When money is tight, people fight about it more. It's like any other limited resource. When there are only two cookies left in the pack, chances are all three kids in the family are going to want one. An argument is the result. There are fewer fights about money, in my experience, when there is enough to go around. Then people give in to their better instincts, the ones that tell them they don't have to be in control of everything.

Another big reason people fight about money? Conflicting priorities. Just because a couple is married, for example, or has been together a really long time, doesn't mean that the two members of that couple have the exact same wants. And in the same way, you and your parents don't have exactly the same wants. That's why I am a big fan of what I like to call financial autonomy: Every person should have some money of his or her own. When *you* have money of your own, then *you* can decide what to do with it.

Whose Money Is It, Anyway?

I get kind of mad at my mom because she won't let me buy stuff. But I think if it's my money, I should be able to spend it on what I want.

—Samantha, 12

When I graduated from college, I moved to New York City. I lived in a small apartment in Brooklyn. This was before DVRs, before iPods, before voice mail. If you weren't around to answer your phone yourself, you needed an answering machine. I didn't have one, and on my salary of $11,000 a year I couldn't afford to buy one. Until one weekend, when I was wandering around downtown and I saw a man selling answering machines on the street for $20. At that price, I told myself, I couldn't afford *not* to buy one.

When I put it in my tote bag, I was surprised at how heavy it was. But I had things to do that day and didn't have time to run it home, so I trudged along. I didn't care. I had just gotten an incredible bargain. And when I got home later that night, I got out my scissors and tore into the box and found . . . a brick.

ANSWERING MACHINE

I hope you're laughing. But I sure wasn't. I know it was only $20, but even $20 was a lot of money to me back then. I felt taken. And I felt stupid. Why am I telling you this story? Because this is why parents try to tell you what to do with your money. They don't want you to do stupid things like buying bricks on the streets of New York City. They don't want you to make any financial mistakes, whether those mistakes cost you $20 or $2,000. They don't want you to do the same dumb things that they did themselves.

So sometimes they make rules about how you can and can't spend your money—whether it's money that they give you or money that you earn. They may do it using a rule about how much of your allowance or birthday money you have to save or give to charity.

Or they may do it like Samantha's parents, by just saying no. Personally, I hope—and you can feel free to show them this page too—that they're giving you at least some, or preferably a lot, of freedom to make your own decisions. Because the best way for you to learn how *not* to waste money is to waste some of your own. Buy a $70 hoodie that goes out of style by the middle of next week. Fork over $50 for a video game that you didn't research enough to realize it was better suited to eight-year-olds. You'll be much more careful and thoughtful about spending your money in the future.

Money, and Right and Wrong

Have you ever heard the term "value judgment"? It's when you decide how you feel about a particular situation based on your own personal values. As I was doing the research for this book, I heard a lot of stories of financial problems that involved value judgments. Take a look, then think about what you'd do in these situations. Even better, talk it over with a friend.

I wanted a new iPod, so I sold my old one to my brother and I cut the price because he's my brother. Anyway, we went somewhere and it got stolen and so did his wallet, so he hasn't paid me for it.

—Blake, 13

QUESTIONS:
- Was Blake's brother right or wrong?
- Should he pay for the iPod?
- Should Blake just let it go?

Say my brother breaks a toy of mine. I say he owes me that money that the toy was worth and he has to pay me back.

—Dino, 11

QUESTIONS:
- Should Dino's brother have to pay for the toy?
- What if Dino didn't buy the toy in the first place, but his parents did?
- What if Dino's brother doesn't have money of his own?

My parents know where I keep my money, so anytime they know they can't pay someone, they just take it. And when I realize that they took my money, I get really mad.

—Stacia, 12

QUESTIONS:
- Do your parents ever take money from you?
- Do they do it without asking—and never pay it back?
- How would you feel if they asked to borrow the money instead?
- What could you say to your parents to make them understand how you feel about this?

The Fun of Giving It Away

I usually donate my old toys and old clothes that I don't use anymore. My brother is a pack rat and doesn't get rid of anything. But I look through my stuff and say, "Do I really need this?" And if it's something I like but I don't really use that much, I give it to someone who might like it more.

—Evan, 13

I usually don't donate money. I go to the Salvation Army and give them clothes and stuff I don't need anymore, like old books.

—Eric, 12

Want your money to make you really happy? Give some away. No, I'm not kidding. People who give back are happier and healthier. They sleep better and exercise more, and that puts them in a better mood. Why? Because gratitude—feeling thankful and giving back—is the opposite of materialism. When you're materialistic, you focus too much of your energies on things that you want, things typically that other people have. It doesn't bring out the best in anyone. When you're grateful, you appreciate what you already have. And if you can look at even those things you're not necessarily grateful for (like the opportunity to go to school) as a gift, you're more likely to focus on how life might be if you didn't have them. And that makes you appreciate them even more.

But—here's the thing—there are more than one million charities in America alone. And chances are, every one of them would like your money or your time as a volunteer. How do you decide which organizations are worth supporting? Here are a few rules of the road:

- **Follow your interests.** Do you have a soft spot for animals? Is there a lot of heart disease or cancer in your family? Or is the environment at the top of your list? Getting involved with charities that deal with any of those issues is just fine. But it's important for you to understand what sorts of charities speak loudest to you. Because as I said earlier, money is a limited resource. Just like you can't buy every thing you want to buy, you can't give money to every charity that asks—or even every charity you'd like to give money to. You'll have to decide which are your priorities. That gives you license to say no to the others.

- **Do some research.** If you know that you'd like to support a charity that fights hunger, or autism, or whatever, but don't know which specific organizations do that, you can find them online. Start at a database called Charity Navigator (www.charitynavigator.org). On the site you can type in the name of the charity that interests you, and the database will spit back a report detailing the group's goals, how well they are doing meeting their goals, and how they're spending their donations. You can read the ratings given to that charity by the folks at Charity Navigator (not all charities are created equal) as well as comments from other donors. Another solid information charity website is www.guidestar.org.
- **One number to watch.** If you go to either of these charity information websites, you'll see what's called a charity's program ratio. This number tells you what percentage of the charity's income goes to its actual programs, as opposed to administrative costs and other overhead. If you compare groups by this number, understand that you should compare apples to apples. You compare the food banks with the food banks, the homeless outreach programs with the homeless outreach programs, and

the museums with other museums. Why? Because some causes naturally incur more administrative costs. A museum, for instance, needs security, a large—and well-positioned—building, insurance, and a cleaning staff. A food bank doesn't.

- **Ask questions.** The people who run any charity in your community should be open to talking to a potential donor. Ask about the group's short-term and long-term goals, how they plan to reach them, and what progress they've made in the past.

- **Think about nonfinancial ways to give.** Just because you don't have enough money to give during a particular week or month doesn't mean that you can't be charitable. There are many free ways to give as well. If you have a few hours a week or month, you might be able to volunteer. If you have used clothing or extra cans of food, donate them. Every little bit helps.

The Last Word

Is this everything that you'll ever need to know about money? Absolutely not. But it's a good start. I hope that it makes you interested enough to want to earn some money, save some money, invest some money, and give some back. If you have questions or are looking for other resources, please visit me at my website: www.jeanchatzky.com. There you may find the answers you're looking for, or you can e-mail me a question at jean@jeanchatzky.com and I'll do my best to get back to you as soon as I possibly can.

APPENDIX A
A SHORT HISTORY OF MONEY

9000 B.C. In the beginning there were cows. Well, not just cows, but sheep and camel. They all came under the heading of "cattle," and cattle—though you couldn't exactly squeeze them into your wallet—were the earliest form of money. They were bartered, or traded, for things that early humans needed: plants, grain, other animals. Interestingly, people bartered either with strangers or with their enemies, not with their friends. They may have been onto something. Haven't you ever heard the expression "Friends and money don't mix"?

1200 B.C. What we learned a long time ago was that although bartering was useful, unfortunately, it wasn't the perfect system. Why? Because not all goods were ready to be brought to market, or swapped, simultaneously. Say you had some sheep and you wanted to trade their wool for some grain. The sheep might be ready for shearing well before the grain was ready for harvest. Or the grain might be ready for harvest, but the sheep might not have enough wool to shear. There was no Internet to create a market where people could keep track of who had what when.

It became apparent that a placeholder was needed—something that, like the bills of today (which, if you think about it, have no value other than the value we give them), could be exchanged for the wool of the sheep, or the meat of the cattle, or the grain from the harvest whenever it happened to be ready, then used to purchase more of those or other goods later on. The first currency to be used this way was something called the cowrie shell, a seashell common in the Pacific and Indian oceans that was used for trading primarily in Africa and Asia. Cowrie shells may look familiar to you if you've ever visited a gift shop in a seashore town.

1000–650 B.C. Seashells? I know what you're thinking. If seashells were still valuable, you'd be a millionaire. You'd go out to the beach on a day when the waves were active and fill up your buckets. Piece of cake. Our ancestors in China hit on the same notion around the year 1000 B.C. They started making copies of cowries out of lumps of metal, usually bronze or copper or another nonprecious metal. These morphed over time and eventually became round disks of metal, sometimes with holes in the middle so that they could be strung, like a

necklace, and easily transported. The problem with these early coins was that they, too, had no value in and of themselves, so it was hard to trade them for valuable goods. That changed around 650 B.C. in Lydia (part of what we call Turkey today), where coins were made from precious metals like silver and gold. They were imprinted with words and pictures, often of gods. And although not every coin was worth the same amount, they could be tested to figure out how much of the precious metal was in each little nugget and, therefore, how valuable it was. They could also be recycled. Eventually the amount of metal in each coin was standardized so that they didn't have to be weighed upon use.

A.D. 806 The problem with using precious metals, or even not-so-precious ones, as the Chinese learned, was that sometimes you couldn't find them (or mine them) when you needed them. The Chinese ran short of the copper they were using for their coins, so they issued first leather money, then paper money. The first paper money was actually a receipt. Coins were deposited in a bank, and the person making that deposit was given a receipt for that amount. That receipt (kind of like a store credit you'd get today) was understood to be just as valuable as the coins in the bank, so eventually people started trading the receipts or bills themselves. The paper money—which wasn't woven of gold or silver—didn't have any intrinsic value or worth. Its value was in the promise, first by the bank, later by the government, to redeem it for coins or precious metal that did have intrinsic value. For instance, the British pound (or pound sterling, as it's sometimes called) was originally backed by a pound of—you guessed it—sterling silver.

1816 The gold standard provided a means by which to value money. Beginning in 1816, the U.S. government was allowed to print money by stockpiling enough gold to back it up. Even this was not without controversy. Gold had people in its corner. But so did silver. Unfortunately for silver's proponents, miners in the western United States continued to discover large amounts of this precious metal. As the supply of something goes up, the price of that item typically goes down. And that's what happened with silver. Because there was more of it, it became less valuable. Eventually—in 1900—the gold standard was adopted by law (a dollar at that time was worth 1.5 grams of gold, and an ounce of gold was worth $20.67), and it remained in effect until the beginning of the 1970s.

1862 The first paper money in the United States was issued on March 10, 1862, in five-dollar, ten-dollar, and twenty-dollar denominations. A year later the National Currency Act made the dollar the sole currency of the United States, getting rid of all earlier forms of money.

1930 The gold standard didn't end until the early 1970s. But it was brought down a notch by president Franklin D. Roosevelt, and the effects of the Great Depression gave it a run for its money. In the late 1920s, much as in the past few years, Americans took on way too much debt. When the stock market **crashed** in 1929 and they couldn't pay back the money, they were forced to sell the **assets** they had borrowed for—things like houses and stocks—at much lower prices. The net worth of individuals and businesses sank, and bankruptcies boomed. What happened next? Banks stopped lending. The American economy shrank, and unemployment went sky-high. People lost confidence that they'd find another job (ever) or rebuild their savings (ever). More importantly, they lost confidence in their banks, some of which were going out of business. So just like in the scene from the movie *It's a Wonderful Life* (which is always on around Christmas), they lined up to pull whatever money they had out of the bank—but they didn't want their money in dollars, they wanted it in something they thought would hold its value better: gold. These tough times in America lasted for years.

1933 When President Roosevelt took office, his first action was to declare a national bank holiday. He closed every bank in the United States for a week and allowed them to reopen only if they were investigated and found to be solvent. This boosted confidence in the banks. To rebuild the faith in the dollar, he made the dollar the only real choice by allowing Americans to own no more than $100 in gold (with the exception of jewelry). As a result, after the Depression and World War II it became more and more difficult to control the value of the dollar by tying it to gold.

So what happened to all the gold? The government seized it, paying owners $20.67 per ounce. (Individuals regained the right to own and trade gold in 1975, and it's worth about fifty-three times that original price today!) The government needed somewhere safe to store all that gold, so the United States Bullion Depository Fort Knox—or simply Fort Knox, as most people call it—was built about thirty miles outside Louisville, Kentucky. Fort Knox accepted its first shipments of gold four years later, in 1937, and continues to hold gold today.

1975 The dollar became a free-floating currency. What does this mean? After the gold standard was abandoned, the dollar and the rest of our currency became what's called fiat money. Unlike commodity money—the value of which is tied to a particular commodity, like gold—fiat money is tied only to the promise of its government. The word "fiat," in fact, comes from Latin and means "let it be done." In other words, a dollar is worth a dollar simply because our government says it is.

HOW MONEY IS MADE

You Wanted to Know:

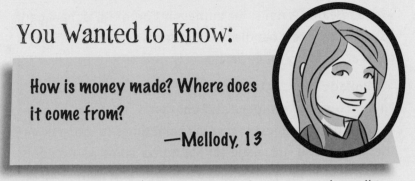

How is money made? Where does it come from?

—Mellody, 13

Well, that depends on what kind of money you're talking about.

Let's start with coins. In 2008 the United States made, or minted, about 10 billion coins for general circulation. In 2009 it produced about 3.5 billion. General circulation coins are those used by people to buy things each and every day—our quarters, nickels, dimes, and pennies. But the U.S. Mint makes other types of coins too:

- **Bullion coins** are purchased by people as investments. They're made from precious metals (gold, silver, or platinum).
- **Commemorative coins** are bought by coin collectors and honor a special person, place, institution, or event.
- **Medals** are awards that honor people, places, institutions, and events for doing something important in areas such as the military and medicine.
- **Regular proof coin sets** contain regular coins (penny, nickel, dime, etc.) that are made by a special, high-quality minting process for collectors to purchase.

In the United States today, there are six different mints. And each does something slightly different.

Washington, DC: The U.S. Mint headquarters. This is where research is done, the entire mint program is managed, customer service is handled, and orders are processed, but no coins are actually made here.

Philadelphia, PA: The largest mint in the world. In Philly, coins are sculpted and engraved, all types of coins are produced (not just for us, but sometimes for other countries), and dies are made for stamping coins and medals. If you're in Philly you can take a tour of the mint. Tours in Philadelphia are self-guided, so there's no need to make a reservation.

West Point, NY: Gold, silver, and platinum bullion are stored here, and commemorative and uncirculated coins are produced—including the 24-karat one-ounce American Buffalo Gold Bullion Coin.

Fort Knox, KY: Right now nearly 150 million ounces of gold are being stored at Fort Knox. Over the years it has also been used to store the U.S. Constitution, the Declaration of Independence, and Abraham Lincoln's Gettysburg Address.

Denver, CO: Here coins are produced, and gold and silver bullion are stored. And you can take a tour as well. Be sure to make a reservation, as these tours book up quickly. To save yourself a spot, visit the U.S. Mint website at www.usmint.gov or call 303-405-4761.

San Francisco, CA: Regular proof and silver proof coin sets and commemorative coins are produced here.

It takes years to get a coin from the planning stages into your pocket. Before a new coin can enter circulation, the secretary of the treasury must first approve the design. Next, models of the coin are made, initially out of wax, then out of plaster. Once a coin is fully designed, blanks in the shapes and sizes of coins are cut from strips of metal. (Pennies are the exception. Instead of *making* the blanks for pennies, the mint *buys* them.) Once the blanks are ready, they're heated, washed in a chemical solution, polished, rinsed, and dried. Then the coins go through what's called the "upsetting" process. You've probably noticed that coins have a raised edge. To make this raised edge, a machine called an upsetting mill takes the coins and raises a rim around the edge of the blank. Finally, new coins are stamped with the appropriate designs on the front and back simultaneously. It takes up to 170 tons of pressure to do this—for reference, 170 tons is the weight of about thirty-four full-grown elephants! Any rejects are thrown back into the melting pot, and the rest are sent to banks.

Bills are another story entirely. The United States produces 38 million bills *every day* at the Bureaus of Engraving and Printing in Washington, DC, and Fort Worth, Texas. Every day 18 tons of ink are used. That's enough to fill about 42,971,908 ballpoint pens.

Why do we need to print so much paper money? Because unlike coins, bills deteriorate. The more they get used, the more quickly they have to come out of circulation. One-dollar bills last about twenty-one months, and one-hundred-dollar bills last about seven and a half years. You've probably had the experience of ripping the corner of a dollar or even tearing one in half.

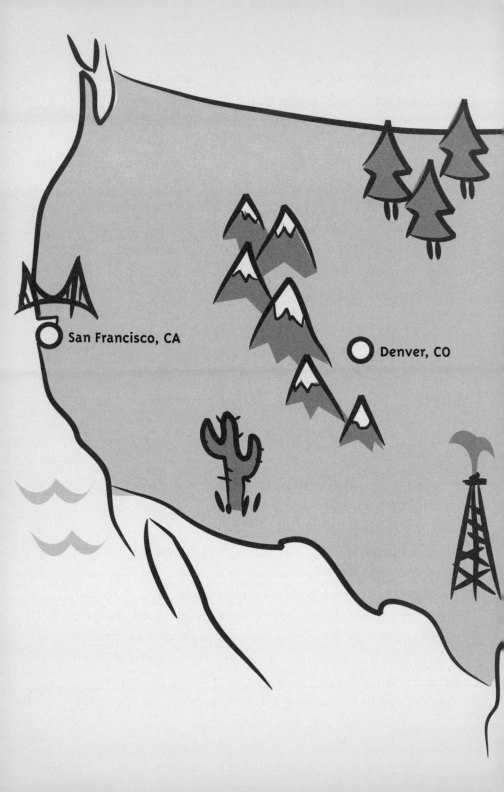

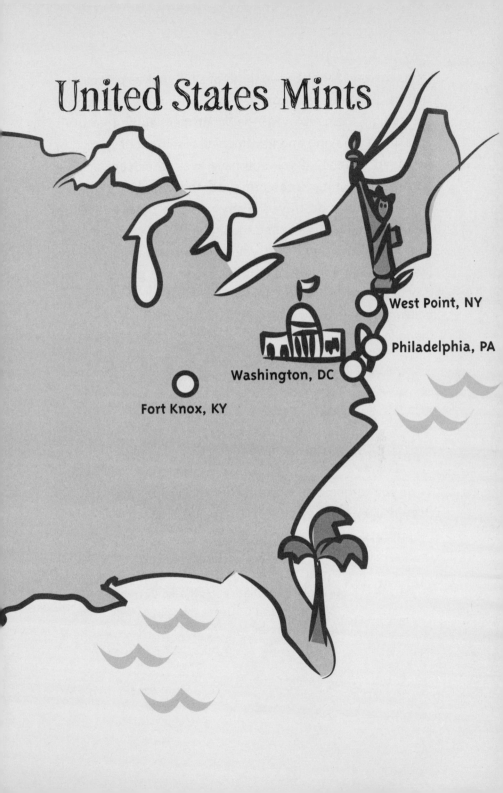

United States Mints

West Point, NY

Philadelphia, PA

Washington, DC

Fort Knox, KY

Or maybe you've gotten two thirds of a bill back as part of your change. What are you supposed to do with those? Sometimes you can get them replaced. The Department of the Treasury's Bureau of Engraving and Printing will take back destroyed or damaged currency if you still have over 50 percent of your damaged bill or if you can prove that the other part of the bill has been totally destroyed. Every year the bureau redeems over $30 million in damaged money. If you have money that you think can be returned, you can mail or deliver it to the Bureau of Engraving and Printing. If you're going to mail it, you'll need to include a letter explaining how the money became damaged. To return the currency by mail, send it to the following address:

> Bureau of Engraving and Printing
> MCD/OFM, BEPA
> Room 344A
> P.O. Box 37048
> Washington, DC 20013

If you're going to make the trip to the bureau yourself (they're open Monday through Friday 8 a.m. to 2 p.m.), here's the address:

> Bureau of Engraving and Printing
> Office of Compliance, Mutilated Currency
> Fourteenth and C streets, SW
> Washington, DC

GLOSSARY

allowance: An amount of money parents give kids to help them learn to manage money. The amount is usually given weekly. Sometimes an allowance is tied to completing responsibilities, such as household chores or jobs for the family.

annual percentage rate (APR): The rate of interest (in terms of a percent, such as 8.75 percent) being charged for a loan over a year's time. The APR includes interest, transaction fees, and service fees.

appreciate: To grow in value. This term is usually used in relation to investments—stocks, collectibles, etc.—that are worth more than you paid for them.

asset: Any item of value that you own, such as a house, land, gems, stocks, bonds, or money in savings.

ATM: Automatic teller machine. An electronic banking station that enables people to take care of banking business twenty-four hours a day, seven days a week. You can deposit and withdraw money, pay loans, etc., at most ATMs.

balance: (1) *In talking about loans*, the balance is the difference between the amount owed and the amount paid. If you pay $45 on a $100 debt, your balance is $55. (2) *In talking about checkbooks*, balancing means to account for all money that came into and went out of your account, so that at the end of the month your check register and your bank statement agree. (3) *In talking about savings*, your balance is what is left in your savings account after you deposit or withdraw money.

bank: A financial institution licensed by a government. Its primary activities include borrowing and lending money.

bond: An IOU issued by a corporation or government that confirms you are lending the corporation or government money. Bonds pay interest regularly to lenders. At the end of the term of the bond, the borrower returns to the lender the face value of the bond (the amount the lender invested in the bond).

budget: A plan you create for controlling spending and encouraging saving.

certificate of deposit (CD): A type of investment that requires you to invest money for a certain length of time and guarantees the same rate of return (interest) for that entire time. CDs usually require a minimum deposit.

charge: To borrow money (from a store, service provider, or credit card company) to make a purchase. If you do not pay the debt off in full within the card issuer's *grace period* (usually twenty-five to twenty-eight days), you will pay interest on the amount you owe.

check register: A small booklet that comes with your checkbook where you can keep track of all the deposits, ATM withdrawals, and checks you write. If you keep your check register up-to-date, you always know how much money you have in your checking account.

collateral: Property used to assure the payment of a loan. In other words, if the borrower does not pay back the loan, the borrower must give up this property or money.

compound interest: Interest on an investment, like a savings account, that is calculated not only on the money you originally invested, but also on any interest the investment has already earned. Compounding can take place annually, semi-annually, quarterly, monthly, or daily. The more often interest is compounded, the faster your money will grow.

corporation: The most common form of organizing a business. The organization's total worth is divided into shares of stock, and each share represents a unit of ownership and is sold to stockholders. A corporation is considered a separate entity from the stockholders for legal and tax purposes. Examples of corporations: PepsiCo, Intel, Gap.

crash: To suffer a downward movement in the market that has lasting effects, particularly on investors' emotions.

credit: A loan that enables people to buy something now and pay for it in the future.

credit limit: The highest amount you may charge on a credit card. Your limit is set by your card company's opinion of your ability to handle debt.

debit card: this plastic card looks like a credit card, but it is used to withdraw money from a savings or checking account. When you use a debit card at ATMs to get cash or in stores to make purchases, money is immediately withdrawn from your account. You cannot withdraw more money than you have in the account.

debt: Money or goods that you owe.

deposit: To put money into a bank or investment account.

depression: A severe, sustained recession.

discount: A reduction from the original price or an item's full worth; on sale.

diversification: The act of spreading out the money you invest into different types of investments: bonds, stocks, CDs, mutual funds, etc. The idea is to avoid putting all your eggs in one basket. Different kinds of investments do well in different kinds of economic climates. Therefore, if one of your investments drops in value, the other kinds of investments should hold or increase their value.

Dow Jones average: The most widely followed index of U.S. markets.

earned income: Wages paid in exchange for work.

earnings statement: A document that acts as a record of your earnings and deductions. If your paycheck is deposited into your bank account electronically, this document is also a record of that transaction.

FDIC: The Federal Deposit Insurance Corporation. Established as

part of the Banking Act of 1933, the FDIC protects bank customers from possible losses by insuring various kinds of savings
accounts up to $250,000 per account.

federal funds rate: The interest rate at which the Federal Reserve
lends money to banks.

Federal Reserve System: The central banking system of the United
States, created in 1913 with the signing of the Federal Reserve
Act by Woodrow Wilson.

FICA: The Federal Insurance Contributions Act tax. This payroll tax
is used to fund Medicare and Social Security.

fixed: Not changing. Fixed interest rates never change during the
time of the investment or loan.

fixed expenses: Expenses that stay basically the same from month
to month, such as housing and transportation.

grace period: The amount of time you have to pay a bill or a loan
in full, usually about twenty-five to twenty-eight days. If you
pay within the grace period, you do not have to pay a finance
charge.

gross domestic product: GDP, as it is called, is the value of all the
goods and services produced in a country. This number is used
to represent the size of the economy.

gross pay: The entire amount of your income or paycheck *before*
any deductions—like taxes or insurance payments—are subtracted.

income tax: Money that wage earners pay the government to run
the country. The amount of the tax depends upon how much
you earn.

inflation: The rate at which prices rise.

insufficient funds: A phrase that means you did not have enough
money to cover an expense. Usually checks that bounce are
returned stamped with the phrase "insufficient funds." The
amount of the check was larger than the balance in the checking account.

insured savings: Accounts that are insured up to $250,000 by the FDIC. Banks are insured by the FDIC, so your money in those bank accounts is insured.

interest: The amount paid by a borrower to a lender for the privilege of borrowing the money.

interest rate: The price paid for the use of someone else's money, expressed as an annual percentage rate, such as 6.5 percent.

invest: To put your money into CDs, money market accounts, mutual funds, savings accounts, bonds, stocks, or objects that you hope will grow in value and earn you more money.

labor force: People over the age of sixteen who have a job or are actively looking for one.

lagging indicator: a signal that the economy has gone up or down. An example of a lagging indicator is unemployment because it rises and falls in response to the economy.

late fee: An amount of money charged to you for missing a payment date. If your payment arrives late or not at all, the charge is added to your debt. Late fees are strong penalties. Credit companies routinely charge $30 or more if you miss your payment date. Get organized!

leading indicator: a signal that tells economists if the economy is headed up or headed down. An example of a leading indicator is the stock market because it rises and falls before the economy does.

liquid: A word used to describe an investment that can be easily turned into cash.

loan: Money or an object that is lent, usually with the understanding that the loan will be paid back with interest.

long-term: For a period of many months or years. An example of long-term savings might be saving to buy a car or pay for college. People invest long-term for retirement, for example.

Medicare: A social insurance program administered by the U.S. government. It provides medical insurance coverage to people age sixty-five and over, or who meet other special criteria.

minimum payment: The smallest amount you are required to pay a lender each month on a debt.

minimum wage: The lowest hourly, daily, or monthly wage that employers are legally allowed to pay their employees.

money market account: A savings account offered by a bank (or a mutual fund). The account typically requires that you make a minimum deposit and that you maintain a minimum balance. The account invests in certificates of deposit and treasury bills and pays a rate of interest that rises and falls with the economy.

mortgage: The money borrowed from a lender to buy property, usually a house. The borrower makes payments on the loan each month until the entire loan, along with interest, is paid in full.

mutual fund: An investment that uses cash from a pool of investors to buy a wide range of securities, like stocks, bonds, and real estate. This is a way to diversify your investments, because you own small units of each of the fund's securities. The fund is managed by professionals and permits small amounts of money to be invested.

net pay: The amount of your income or paycheck *after* any deductions—like taxes or insurance payments—are subtracted. This is your take-home pay.

overdraft: The act of withdrawing more money from an account than is available in the account. You write a check for $25, but your account contains only $20. You will have to pay the bank a penalty charge for going over the limit.

percentage: A part of a whole expressed in hundredths. The whole amount is divided into 100 smaller, but equal, parts, each called a percent. Therefore, 6 percent is 6 units out of 100 percent (the whole). If you have invested $100 and you earn 8 percent interest on the money, you will earn 8 parts of the whole, or $8.

principal: The amount of money you borrow in a loan. You pay this back plus interest.

profit: The money you've earned after you subtract (a) any money you had to spend to make the product or perform the service, and (b) any taxes that had to be paid on your earnings.

recession: The slowing down of economies during a sustained period of time. Gross domestic product (GDP), employment, investment spending, capacity utilization, household incomes, and business profits all fall during a recession.

return: The amount of money a saver receives from a savings account or fund. The return is usually expressed as a percentage, as in "This account returns 7.37 percent."

risk: The likelihood that you will lose money on an investment.

save: To hang on to your money for a future use instead of spending it. Saving is the opposite of spending.

savings account: A bank account that pays you interest for keeping your savings in it. Banks use your money to make loans, so they pay you interest for the use of your money. Your savings are insured up to $250,000 by the FDIC, so you don't have to worry about borrowers taking your money and not paying it back.

securities: Securities are instruments (i.e. things) you invest in that can be exchanged or sold. Broadly, there are two different types of securities—equity securities, or stocks, and debt securities, or bonds—though there are many different securities that fall into those categories and others that mix the two.

share: A unit of ownership in an investment or a company.

shareholder: Someone who owns stock in a company.

short-term: For a period of days, weeks, or a few months. Short-term savings are for something you know you will need to pay for soon, like a new iPod. Short-term investing usually means choosing an investment that is liquid, meaning you can pull your money out easily.

Social Security: A program of the U.S. government that gives money to elderly people. The elderly receive funds because the federal government has deducted a tax from each of their paychecks during the course of their working lives. The money taken out of their paychecks has been deposited into the Social Security Trust Fund. Employers, too, deposited money into this fund on behalf of each employee. When people reach a certain age, they become eligible to receive Social Security payments. The government mails checks each month. These payments help the elderly live, now that they are no longer working full-time. The money they receive is drawn out of the Social Security Trust Fund, where it has been earning interest for many years.

stock market: A market is a public place where things are bought and sold. The term "stock market" refers to the business of buying and selling stock. The stock market is not a specific place, though some people use the term "Wall Street"—the main street in New York City's financial district—to refer to the U.S. stock market in general. It is an organized way for people to buy and sell stocks, and for corporations to raise money. There are three widely known stock exchanges: the New York Stock Exchange, the American Stock Exchange, and the National Association of Securities Dealers Automated Quotations system (you hear it called NASDAQ on the news).

tax: A sum of money that is demanded by a government for its support, or for specific facilities or services, and is levied upon incomes, property, sales, etc.

tax evasion: The nonpayment of taxes, as through the failure to report taxable income.

unearned income: Money earned that is not the result of labor, such as interest from a savings account or other kind of investment.

variable expenses: Expenses that can be controlled and typically change from month to month. For example, groceries can be a variable expense. You can choose to buy expensive food (steak, lobster, lamb chops, or shrimp) or inexpensive food (chicken legs, turkey, hamburger). With variable expenses, you have choices.

withdrawal: The act of taking money out of an account.

WEB RESOURCES

If you'd like to learn more about your money, check out these websites.

- H.I.P. Pocket Change
  www.usmint.gov/kids
  Games, cartoons, and puzzles help you understand the history of money.
- Savings Quest, by Wells Fargo
  www.mysavingsquest.com
  This game lets you pick a job, manage your income, meet savings goals, and pay for the things you want and need.
- Investing for Kids
  http://library.thinkquest.org/3096
  Designed for kids by kids, this website explains the basics of investing your money—including stocks, bonds, and mutual funds.
- KidsBank.com by Sovereign Bank
  www.kidsbank.com
  Explore the fundamentals of banking in a fun and interactive way.
- BuckInvestor.com
  www.buckinvestor.com
  This site covers the ins and outs of investing and saving, written in an easy-to-understand way.
- YoungBiz
  www.youngbiz.com
  Learn how to make smart financial and business decisions using skills you already have.

- Fed 101
  www.federalreserveeducation.org/fed101
  Get an interactive look at the Federal Reserve system,
  including the life of a dollar bill.
- Escape from Knab: The Adventure, by U.S. Bank
  www.escapefromknab.com
  You land on foreign planet Knab and discover the next
  rocket back to Earth is quite expensive. To pay your
  fare, you need to work and save money. Good luck!
- Consumer Jungle
  www.consumerjungle.org
  Learn how to avoid common financial mistakes and
  scams.
- Money $marts, by Girl Scouts of the USA
  www.girlscouts.org/moneysmarts
  This site offers ideas for how to earn, save, spend, and
  invest your money.
- High School Financial Planning Program, by the
  National Endowment for Financial Education
  http://hsfpp.nefe.org/students
  Learn the difference between good and bad debt, and
  how to budget, invest, and plan for your career.
- TeenAnalyst
  www.teenanalyst.com
  This site provides investment tips and advice for teens.
- Hands on Banking, by Wells Fargo
  www.handsonbanking.org
  Learn how to make the most of your money and bud-
  get wisely.
- The Wall Street Journal Classroom Edition
  http://classroomedition.com/cre
  Read money news in terms you can understand.

ABOUT THE AUTHOR

JEAN CHATZKY is the bestselling author of a number of books, including *Money 911*, *Pay It Down!*, *You Don't Have to Be Rich*, and *Make Money, Not Excuses*. She is the financial editor for the *Today* show and has been on the *Oprah Winfrey Show* many times. Jean's writing has appeared in *USA Weekend*, *Time*, *Money*, and the New York *Daily News*. She has two children and lives in Westchester County, New York.